MEASURING THE VALUE OF CORPORATE PHILANTHROPY:

SOCIAL IMPACT, BUSINESS BENEFITS, AND INVESTOR RETURNS

by

Terence Lim, Ph.D.

Preface

How to measure the value and results of corporate philanthropy remains one of corporate giving professionals' greatest challenges. Social and business benefits are often long-term or intangible, which make systematic measurement complex. And yet: Corporate philanthropy faces increasing pressures to show it is as strategic, cost-effective, and value-enhancing as possible. The industry faces a critical need to assess current practices and measurement trends, clarify the demands practitioners face for impact evidence, and identify the most promising steps forward in order to make progress on these challenges.

This report aims to meet that need, by providing the corporate philanthropic community with a review of recent measurement studies, models, and evidence drawn from complementary business disciplines as well as the social sector. Rather than present another compendium of narrative accounts and case studies, we endeavor to generalize the most valuable concepts and to recognize the strengths and limitations of various measurement approaches. In conjunction with the annotated references that follow, the analysis herein should provide an excellent starting point for companies wishing to adapt current methodologies in the field to their own corporate giving programs.

To realize meaningful benefits, philanthropy cannot be treated as just another "check in the box," but rather must be executed no less professionally, proactively, and strategically than other core business activities. Our hope is that this work will enlighten giving professionals, CEOs, and the investor community to the many mechanisms by which philanthropic investments can be measured and managed to achieve long-term business value and meet critical societal needs.

Terence Lim, Ph.D.
Report Author and Manager, Standards and Measurement
Committee Encouraging Corporate Philanthropy
(through the 2008–2009 Goldman Sachs Public Service Program)

TABLE OF CONTENTS

Introduction

Corporate philanthropy is as vital as ever to business and society, but it faces steep pressures to demonstrate that it is also cost-effective and aligned with corporate needs.[1] Indeed, many corporate giving professionals cite measurement as their primary management challenge.[2] Social and business benefits are often long-term, intangible, or both, and a systematic measurement of these results can be complex. Social change takes time. The missions and intervention strategies involved are diverse. For these reasons, the field of corporate philanthropy has been unable to determine a shared definition or method of measurement for social impact. Similarly, the financial value of enhancing intangibles such as a company's reputational and human capital cannot be measured directly and may not be converted into tangible, bottom-line profits in the near term. Corporate givers and grant recipients often use less formal, anecdotal methods to convey impact. While stories may vitalize and publicize a program's successes, it is more systematic measurement that brings rigor and discipline to the field. Data-based evidence quantifies the positive effects of corporate philanthropy, thus making a more persuasive case for why companies should engage in philanthropic causes.

If corporate philanthropy is to make progress in meeting these challenges, the industry must meaningfully assess current practices and measurement trends, clarify precisely what is needed in terms of impact evidence, and then identify the most promising and practical steps forward. This report is designed to aid that critical agenda.

Interviews with senior corporate management and giving professionals revealed a set of common questions they often face. These questions fall naturally into a hierarchy of three conversations:

CONVERSATION ONE. Between grant recipients and their corporate funder's Chief Giving Officer (CGO). The funder wants to know:

- How to assess whether grantees are achieving the intended results, and

- How to estimate a "return on investment" (ROI) numeric for comparing and/or aggregating the effectiveness across different grants in achieving social results.

CONVERSATION TWO. Between the CGO and Chief Executive Officer (CEO).

- When pressing the CEO for significant commitment to philanthropic programs, the CGO is often asked to articulate a "business case" and demonstrate how supporting the philanthropic initiative will be valuable to business.

CONVERSATION THREE. Between the CEO and the investor community.

- Investors want assurance that spending on corporate philanthropy enhances (or at least does not diminish) shareholder value.
- Concurrently, a growing number of investors ask that the companies in which they invest demonstrate greater philanthropic leadership and social responsibility.

Indeed, investors increasingly esteem companies that demonstrate strong social performance, believing that this represents management quality and valuable intangibles. The ability to attract a large base of investors lowers costs of capital and raises share-price valuations, which in turn should incentivize companies to cultivate sustainable philanthropic programs that meet society's critical needs.

The question is: How? Advanced by sophisticated private foundations and governmental agencies, a wide range of impact-assessment methodologies already exists in the social sector. This report examines how some of these methodologies may be applied to the specific needs and motivations of corporate givers, programs, and grants. A wide review of academic and industry literature on the link between corporate social performance and financial performance reinforces the idea that philanthropic initiatives create long-term financial value by enhancing a company's employee engagement, customer loyalty, reputational capital, and market opportunities. But these benefits accrue as intangible assets rather than as short-term cash flows and thus are more complex to measure; moreover, the mechanisms involved have not yet been well-researched and understood. Consequently, some companies pay little attention to assessing philanthropy's financial returns; their engagement is primarily motivated by wanting to meet community obligations and "do the right thing."[3] By analyzing complementary disciplines such as human resources, marketing, risk management, and capital budgeting, corporate philanthropy can improve its measurement methods and identify long-term financial benefits.

The next three parts of this report present in greater detail the conversations summarized above, along with our analyses thereof. The last section presents conclusions as well as recommendations for how industry members might best proceed. An extensive glossary, references, and annotated bibliography follow.

---

1 See The Future of Corporate Philanthropy (*Business Week*, 2008, December 8).

2 A survey of 77 multinational companies conducted by The Conference Board (2006) found that more than one-third of responding companies cite measuring results and outcomes as the biggest challenge they will face in managing their corporate contributions programs.

3 Center on Philanthropy at Indiana University (2007), p. 22.

CONVERSATION ONE.
Between grant recipients and the Chief Giving Officer (CGO)

The nonprofit sector employs a broad range of frameworks, tools, and methodologies to measure the social impact of programs and grants.[1] Many of these approaches have evolved through application by sophisticated private foundations and government agencies, reflecting these organizations' own unique preferences, priorities, and social values. Companies are encouraged to assess whether these approaches can be applied to corporate giving programs.

Corporate givers generally demonstrate two types of philanthropic motivation.[5] The first is a response to community obligations and may characterize an employee- or community-directed grant or volunteer program not necessarily aligned with any strategic giving objective. The second motivation seeks to define and differentiate the company through large, visible signature programs that tackle critical issues, perhaps even on a global scale. These programs typically involve the approval and engagement of senior executives, multi-year partnerships with nonprofit organizations, and (in addition to cash) non-cash contributions such as in-kind products and access to company expertise, training, and connections. When evaluating grant requests or designing signature programs, corporate funders seek to engage nonprofit partners in developing more systematic ways to assess whether the intended results are being achieved and how effectiveness across multiple grants can be aggregated and compared.

> Measurement should be viewed as a process whereby the greatest value is achieved through organizations building up and learning from data and evidence over time.

Financial statements are expressed in common and objective monetary units, but social results are much more varied, subjective, and abstract. A review of measurement methodologies did not turn up a "silver bullet" or single numeric against which performance can be universally gauged. Rather, this reading reinforced the notion that, to an extent, measurement is its own reward. It encourages improvement, management, and the explicit formulation of assumptions and expectations. Measurement should be viewed as a process whereby the greatest value is achieved through organizations building up and learning from data and evidence over time.

Question 1.
How to assess whether grantees are achieving intended results?

The most basic forms of performance metrics comprise two categories. These are "activities," such as the number of staff trained or amount of goods purchased, and "outputs," such as the number of clients served, products distributed, and areas reached. With respect to giving programs comprising primarily short-term, one-off grants driven by community obligations, simply identifying activities and measuring output may be all that is feasible.

However, output and activity metrics alone cannot indicate that positive societal changes are being achieved or if unintended harm is being caused. In the case of program initiatives such as signature projects, companies share a strong connection with the cause and are concerned about the social outcomes of their efforts. Managers of these programs and their nonprofit partners must articulate the process by which changes and results are expected to occur. They should outline clearly how success is defined and track whether and how the programs are affecting their beneficiaries.

Jeffrey Brach, Thomas Tierney, and Nan Stone (2008) of The Bridgespan Group address how nonprofit organizations can meet the mounting pressures they face from funders to demonstrate the effectiveness of their programs. They recount cases of several successful nonprofits' "journey from aspirations to impact" and suggest that nonprofit and program leaders rigorously answer the following interdependent questions:

1. What are the results for which we will hold ourselves accountable?
2. How will we achieve them?
3. What will they really cost?
4. How do we build the organization we need to deliver these results?

The classic article by John Sawhill and David Williamson (2001) of The Nature Conservancy provides another constructive account of the journey of a nonprofit organization toward developing its model for assessing mission success. For decades, The Nature Conservancy had measured advancement toward its goal—conserving biodiversity by protecting the land and water that rare species need to survive—by adding up the value of all charitable donations received and land acreage acquired. These indicators, known as "bucks and acres," "enjoyed strong organizational support, and quite frankly, made us look good," according to Sawhill and Williamson, but there lurked a nagging question as to whether these input and output metrics represented actual progress. The Conservancy decided then to develop a new measurement system, the centerpiece of which was a list of 98 leading indicators of state program performance. However, when the Conservancy tried to implement a pilot test, it collapsed under its own weight. Field staff and managers complained about the laborious record-keeping and glut of information; moreover, they had no way of judging which measures were most important and felt that the system was biased against smaller, resource-poor programs.

Lessons the Conservancy took away from this experience include:

1. Links among the mission, programs, and measures must be clearly defined and articulated in order to narrow the number of required indicators.
2. The measures should be easily collectible and communicable.
3. The measures should be strategically designed and applicable across the organization at all levels, while also encouraging of operating units to focus on high-level strategies.
4. Above all, the measures must address progress toward the mission and illustrate whether and how the organization's actions make a difference.

The Conservancy settled on two impact measures that it believed could serve as surrogates for mission success: biodiversity health and threat abatement. The first was straightforward and could be assessed through regular evaluation of the organisms the Conservancy was trying to protect, using existing scientific surveys as a point of comparison. The second measure, which had to account for the inconsistent nature of biodiversity health and threats, assessed the extent to which the Conservancy identified and devised strategies to abate critical threats at each site.

Grantees, nonprofit partners, and corporate philanthropic programs are more likely to be successful if they address these questions at the outset. Developing a theory of change and explaining how the program will achieve its intended impact are critical components of this preparatory work.

To consider a specific example: The use of bednets helps reduce the transmission of malaria in endemic communities—and Figure 1 illustrates a theory of change (often also called a "logic model") for bednet distribution programs commonly applied in malaria-prevention work.

Figure 1: Logic Model of Bednet-Distribution Program for Malaria Prevention

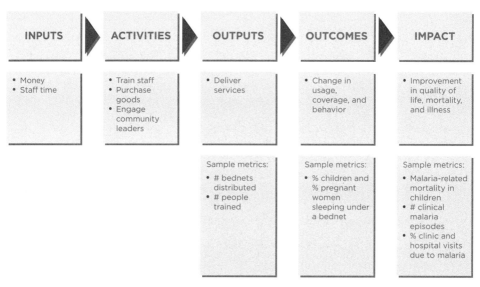

Source: Adapted from McLaughlin C., Levy, J., Noonan, K., & Rosqueta, K. (February 2009).

To further clarify the language of measurement: "outcomes" are those benefits or changes realized as a direct result of a program's activities and other outputs while "impact" refers to long-term results and ultimate social value. Ideally, one could measure along the entire chain of results, from initial activities through intermediate outcomes to final impact, and prove that the program directly resulted in the changes observed.

> Monitoring near-term outcomes can identify opportunities for mid-stream improvements.

In practice, however, the rigorous evaluation of impact is complicated twofold. First, it often takes a long time before final impact can be observed and this involves a lengthy measurement process. Second, one must establish statistically validated causality between services and observed impact in order to prove without doubt that the program in question is responsible. To gauge a grant's success, corporate funders may use other assessment approaches that may be less precise but more timely and practical. Ranked from most-to-least precise, common measurement approaches can be grouped into three categories:

1. **Formal impact evaluations.** Commissioning formal program studies is often the only way to measure and prove the impact arising from a grant. Many such impact studies are expensive and rigid, requiring significant data and a control group (i.e., of participants who do not receive the program's treatments) to be statistically reliable.

2. **Outcomes-measurement systems.** Measuring intermediate outcome metrics may be a practical alternative to formal impact evaluations. Monitoring near-term outcomes can identify opportunities for mid-stream improvements. Applying the models and results of other, already-existing studies can project impact. Definitive causation and attribution are not formally proved, but evidence from other similar treatments may be sufficient to establish that a reasonable link exists between the measured outcomes and ultimate impact.

3. **Assessment of the organization's impact-achievement potential.** With respect to some grants, corporate funders may choose not to be involved in the design or management of the program or measurement process, relying instead entirely on the grantee organization's own metrics, data, and standards. In the social sector, evaluation experts have proposed standardized criteria for assessing

Figure 2: Characteristics of Three Measurement Approaches

Measurement Approach			
	Formal Impact Evaluation	Outcomes Measurement	Impact-Achievement Potential Assessment
What outcome metrics are measured?	Long-term impact as well as intermediate outcomes.	Intermediate outcomes.	Outcome and/or output metrics, which rely upon the grantee organization's own theory of change and measurement standards (funder assesses the organization's potential to achieve impact according to its claims).
How are outcome metrics designed and tracked?	Draws from knowledge and experience of third-party domain-area experts engaged to collect (and/or supervise the collection of) data and then to conduct evaluation analysis.	The corporate funder participates in designing the program and its measurement process, partnering with grantee organizations. Domain-area experts may be consulted. Data is collected and analyzed in-house by the grantee with the corporate partner's technological and/or management assistance.	Self-reported by grantee organization.
How is impact measured?	Long-term impact results are measured and attributed.	May be estimated by applying a model based on assumptions or other evidence about the expected effectiveness of the intervention.	Estimates or actual measures of impact may be available from grantee's measurement process.
What serves as the counter-factual comparison? (i.e., evidence of what would occur if not for the program)	Typically, a comparison group is tracked, often using rigorous experimental design techniques such as Randomized Control Trials (RCTs).	Externally collected national or regional datasets can be used to calculate comparison benchmarks with similar characteristics as the target groups.	Grantee organization's own research may provide comparable measures and demographics from external publications to proxy as benchmarks.
To which programs should the approach be applied?	1. Reasonably mature programs that represent an innovative solution and wherein the funder and/or grantee seeks to prove to other funders or NGOs that it should be scaled-up. 2. Programs wherein the cost and risk of failure is high (e.g., those with highly vulnerable beneficiaries).	1. Programs wherein the funder is involved in the program's design and management and shares responsibility for its success. 2. Programs wherein funders and grantees desire frequent and early indicators in order to make real-time adjustments to interventions and strategy.	1. Start-up programs in their early stages of maturity and stability. 2. Programs wherein the funder is not involved in the program's design or management.

Conversation between grantees and CGO

an organization's potential for achieving measurable and improvable impact. Such assessment can increase confidence among funders that a nonprofit is effecting positive change according to its claims. High-performing characteristics include capable leadership, clear objectives, diligent quality-data collection and analysis, and the informed adjustment of processes to improve.

Choosing which approach or combination of approaches to adopt depends partly on how much confidence funders require in measurement precision and data quality:

• The rigor of formal evaluation places the greatest demand on the quality of underlying data. It also requires the most time. If grantmakers need to make timely decisions, it may be more practical to choose and measure a proximate set of nearer-term outcome indicators believed to be predictors of ultimate impact.

• Programs that are not yet mature or stable may not be ready for formal evaluation, as their theory and implementation are still evolving. In evaluations, treatments cannot be changed without invalidating the test, while control group participants cannot receive the program's services.

• Other evidence, such as the social science literature, may already prove that similar types of interventions work well in certain contexts. Regarding programs designed largely around evidence-based processes, outcomes measurement and/ or impact-potential assessment can reasonably demonstrate that they are on track.

• Existing national and regional datasets can be identified to construct reasonable comparison benchmarks in lieu of formal control groups. (For example, an extensive collection of regional and worldwide statistics on the prevalence of obesity by age, gender, ethnicity, and other population characteristics already exists—and therefore can inform an assessment of programs addressing the obesity issue.)

• For programs wherein the corporate funder is actively involved in design and management, it is worthwhile to implement outcomes-measurement systems or conduct a formal impact-evaluation study when the program becomes more mature.

• If the risk and costs of failure are high, such as when beneficiaries are very vulnerable and the program untested, a formal evaluation may make sense to ensure the program is not causing unintended harm.

• When a program is innovative and stable and the funder is seeking to attract other funders or Non-Governmental Organizations (NGOs) in order to replicate or expand it, it may be time to generate independent proof and attribution, as well as to measure the program's broader effects through formal evaluation.

Figure 3 suggests a decision-making map whereby program managers may choose the best measurement approach for them. Here, the choice can be seen as depending on the motivation for giving and on the confidence needed in the precision of results and quality of data.

Figure 3: Measurement Approaches and Motivation for Grant

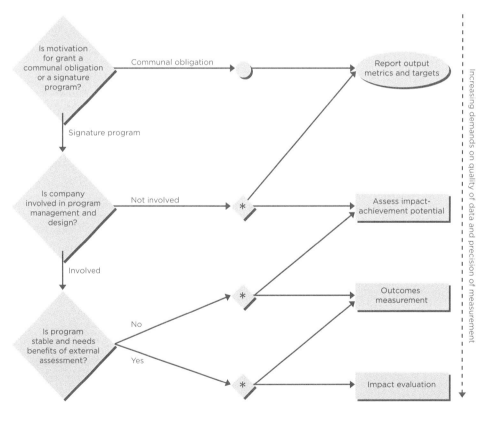

Decision branch to take depends, in part, on confidence needed of measurement precision and data quality.

Conversation between grantees and CGO

Impact evaluation

Formal impact evaluations seek to measure evaluation points along the result chain and prove whether the program under review has been effectual. Independent evaluators who possess domain and analytical expertise are usually engaged, as they bring unbiased knowledge and credibility to the analysis. An evaluator designs the methodology for gathering and analyzing data, taking into consideration factors such as sample sizes, potential biases, and how to establish a control group. Once implemented, the program collects data until a sufficient sample size has accumulated. Then, sophisticated statistical tools analyze the data for evidence of attribution. Finally, an evaluation report is drawn up and presented to stakeholders. The detailed quantitative analysis contained therein is designed to satisfy a high burden of statistical proof: proof of positive impact in the treatment group and that is not found in the control group.

Because formal evaluations employ the highest level of precision and rigor— as well as the engagement of a credible, external evaluator—they can be relatively lengthy, costly, and/or complex. Planning and budgeting in advance is imperative. At the same time, formal evaluations are inherently retrospective, to an extent; after all, results cannot be reasonably anticipated until a program is underway and often not confirmed until completion or long thereafter. Evaluations can be disagreeably rigid in many situations because there is little room, if any, for mid-course methodology adjustment—which could invalidate the data already collected.[6]

Formal evaluations remain a staple of the social sector when program effectiveness must be demonstrated meticulously. Requiring program stability and a high quality of data, formal evaluations are more suited to mature programs. Funders and grantees should discuss at the outset whether the evaluation's potential benefits will justify the expenditure of resources involved. Programs that strategically and innovatively address a social issue are good candidates for independent evaluations because the evaluation can prove attribution and credibly demonstrate to additional funders or NGOs that the programs are worth replicating or expanding. Also good candidates are programs whose cost and risk of failure are high, such as when the targeted beneficiaries are extremely vulnerable. In such cases, "negative" results that discourage continuing the program are of equal or even greater informational value than "positive" ones.

Outcomes measurement

Outcomes-measurement approaches track intermediate changes that are linked to ultimate impact. One example of the social sector's progress with this approach is United Way of America, which emphasizes the importance of outcomes and provides its own local chapters with advice summarized in a guidebook entitled *Measuring Program Outcomes: A Practical Approach and Focusing on Outcome*. Another approach has been jointly developed by The Urban Institute and The Center for What Works (December 2006) to assist nonprofit organizations in developing new outcomes-monitoring processes and/or improving their existing systems. This approach consists of a general framework for identifying common outcome indicators and sector-specific metrics applicable to fourteen program areas.

Although outcomes measurement encourages a focus on results, this approach alone cannot declare definitively whether a program is actually effecting change. Outcomes measurement may involve before-and-after measurement techniques, but not the randomized designs or control groups needed as counterfactual comparisons for formal proofs. Still, whether the program is achieving its intended results can be determined, to an extent, according to the following logic:

1. Existing national and regional datasets can serve as reasonable comparison benchmarks.

2. Related evaluation studies or social science research offer corroborating evidence.

3. There already exists a considerable amount of confidence in the quality of the program's theory of change.

4. The measured data align with judgments suggested by close knowledge of the grantee and interactions with the program's beneficiaries.

Outcomes measurement may generate information on a quarterly or more frequent basis, thus providing funders and grantees with almost real-time information about the project's progress. Used as part of performance management, this approach allows grantees to make mid-stream improvements to their intervention based on the latest data. Often, results are managed in a kind of "dashboard," e.g., an array of charts depicting the project's performance according to a variety of metrics, over time and relative to targets. Giving even more structure to the process, some performance-management systems integrate quality-control concepts already established by business management: these include the "Balanced Scorecard"[7] and "Six Sigma"[8] principles. Corporate givers are especially apt to assist nonprofits in outcomes measurement because they can draw on company-wide experience in devising metrics, collecting data in a disciplined manner, and drawing appropriate conclusions to recommend action.

> Corporate givers are especially apt to assist nonprofits in outcomes measurement because they can draw on company-wide experience in devising metrics, collecting data in a disciplined manner, and drawing appropriate conclusions to recommend action.

The specific logic model and performance metrics that should be implemented in an outcomes-measurement approach are best developed jointly by the program's funder and grantees. The grantee organization knows its own infrastructure and local conditions and this knowledge is complemented by domain expertise and familiarity with the broader social sector. For the benefit of certain causes and strategies already well-researched and evaluated, NGOs, research organizations, and funders have collaborated to endorse a set of common core outcomes and impact metrics.

Including the grantee in the process of devising a measurement framework contributes to a greater sense of partnership and leverages grantee-domain expertise; sometimes grantees even take the lead in defining data collection and measurement design. Allowing the grantee this flexibility reduces the burden of responding to different funders who ask frequently for the same basic information. Moreover, a partnership approach gives grantees a greater sense of ownership—and makes their decision-makers more likely to act on results. Throughout program implementation, the logic model may be re-examined and modified based on the latest data available. According to the W. K. Kellogg Foundation: "The process [of developing a model] is an iterative one. ... Gaps in activities, expected outcomes, and theoretical assumptions can be identified, resulting in changes being made." As Sonal Shah, director of the White House Office of Social Innovation and Civic Participation, has said: "Just like business, which sometimes needs to course-correct, nonprofits and social business should be able to course-correct and make changes. They should only be considered a failure if they fail to correct the problem."[9]

Outcomes measurement tracks the social changes a program targets, but the tracked metrics appear early along the results chain. To estimate ultimate impact, one can apply a model drawn from external evidence and adjusted to current local conditions pertaining to ultimate effectiveness. This external evidence includes quantitative data from prior studies and consultations with sector experts.

To expand on the earlier example of bednet distribution for malaria prevention: Figure 4 outlines how an estimate of impact results (e.g., number of child lives saved) can be calculated by tracking a key outcome indicator. This indicator might be the additional number of children that now use bednets. Evaluators then make informed assumptions about the relevant demographics and anticipated effectiveness of treatment based on prior observations and studies adjusted for local conditions.

Figure 4: Example of a Model for Estimating the Impact of Bednet Distribution

Measure intermediate outcomes		Estimate affected population		Estimate real-world conditions		Estimate tool effectiveness		Estimate impact
Change in coverage (additional % of children that use bednets)	X	Predicted number of deaths and illnesses in community from malaria	X	Influence of human behavior	X	Protective effect under ideal conditions	=	Number of child lives saved
e.g., 80% of population use bednets after program	X	e.g., 13.5/1000 rural children die each year	X	e.g., bednets are used correctly only 65% of the time	X	e.g., bednets are 50% effective when used correctly	=	e.g., 3.5/1000 rural children saved

Source: Adapted from McLaughlin, C., Levy, J., Noonan, K., & Rosqueta, K. (February 2009).

Assessing impact-achievement potential

For grants in which the corporate funder is not involved in program design or management, the funder may choose to rely on the grantees' own measurement process, standards, and data. The funder typically asks grantees to self-report regularly on the following information:

1. What results they are committed to achieve;

2. What measurable evidence will be provided to verify success;

Conversation between grantees and CGO

3. What baseline results will serve as a point of comparison for the new data; and

4. How the grantee will track results and adjust methodology mid-course.

When results are self-reported, assessing impact-achievement potential in a way that also measures general organization capabilities can increase funders' confidence that the organization is achieving the outcomes it claims. As an example of standardized ratings criteria for assessing impact potential, the Alliance for Effective Social Investing has developed and proposed the "Outcome Potential Assessment" framework. Their framework assumes that, regardless of what the nonprofit intends to achieve, there are certain organizational characteristics that tell an investor whether the organization is likely to accomplish its goals. For instance, if an organization does not have a theory of change, or does not diligently collect quality data supporting its effectiveness, or does not use the data it does collect to improve, the organization is unlikely to succeed. Using this framework, nonprofit organizations are rated according to their diligence and acumen in collecting, interpreting, and using data to improve services at the organizational level. Comparisons should be confined to

Methodology for the Alliance for Effective Social Investing's Social Value Assessment Tool

To determine an organization's capacity and potential to deliver high social value, the Alliance for Effective Social Investing (2009) proposes that analysts use a Social Value Assessment Tool, which comprises 26 questions and scores organizations against six indicators:

• Diligence in collecting data.

• Possession of a clear set of outcomes and a logic model that together describe how the organization intends to achieve the desired outcomes.

• Relation of efforts (outputs) to outcomes, to determine whether the organization's intervention is indeed producing the observed outcomes.

• Flexibility in adjusting the service approach given the latest data and changing circumstances.

• Substantiation of the value of the program through data collection and analysis.

• Capacity to deliver program services as they were designed.

Source: Alliance for Effective Social Investing (2009).

organizations working toward comparable outcomes with similar populations. Charity Navigator, the largest charity evaluator in the country, is looking to adopt[10] such an assessment framework so that its final ratings will not just evaluate a charity's financial performance, but also take into account its potential to achieve intended outcomes.

High impact-potential organizations must invest in tools, training, and operational resources needed for measurement. Corporate funders may rely on grantees' own measurement processes, but should also bear in mind that a quality measurement process is vital to achieving impact value and should always be budgeted at the source.

Summary

"Activities" and "output" metrics and targets are the most basic set of trackable performance measures. (In programs comprising short-term, one-off grants, activities and output metrics might very well be the *only* trackable measures.) By themselves, however, output metrics offer little indication that social change is being achieved or unintended harm caused. The three measurement approaches outlined above summarize options for assessing the success of programs wherein corporate givers are concerned about achieving social impact. Formal evaluations (approach 1) are the only way to prove rigorously that an impact is the result of an organization's efforts and therefore validates a logic model. Outcomes measurement (approach 2) focuses on nearer-term changes that allow real-time adjustments to the intervention strategy and logic model in place and provide indications that the program itself is causing the desired outcomes. Impact-achievement potential assessment (approach 3) helps to determine whether an organization has high-performing characteristics that will increase the likelihood that self-reported outcomes are being deliberately achieved. These three approaches are not necessarily exclusive; they can be combined. For example, a young program may still be evolving strategically; its processes may not yet be stable enough to withstand outcomes measurement or formal impact assessment. The organization's *potential* for achieving impact should still be assessed, however—and as the program matures it may become worthwhile to develop processes by which more precise measurement of actual impact may be applied as well.

Question 2.
How to measure the return on social investment from grants and giving programs?

Return on investment (ROI) is a highly favored business concept. Given a standardized ratio of financial benefits-to-costs, decision-makers can gauge how well a project is performing overall, compare the project's efficiency to alternatives, and even aggregate ROIs across multiple projects.

There has also been enthusiasm particularly among sophisticated private foundations for applying ROI techniques to measure the social efficiency of philanthropic programs. In a study commissioned by the Bill & Melinda Gates Foundation, Melinda Tuan (2008) performed a critical review of eight selected approaches for integrating cost into the measurement of social value creation and noted that all of these different methodologies essentially reflected one concept: expected return.

$$\text{Expected Return} = \frac{(\text{Outcome or Benefit x Probability of Success})}{\text{Cost}}$$

A major difference among methodologies is whether benefits are monetized. Methodologies in which benefits are monetized are classically described as *cost-benefit analysis*. Methodologies in which benefits are not monetized are called *cost-effectiveness analysis*. Measurement ratios based on cost-effectiveness are easier to implement and require fewer data assumptions, because they sidestep the challenge of having to convert different aspects of program benefits into common monetary units. However, they can only account for one area of program impact at a time, since impact for different program causes may be measured only in their programs' respective natural units (e.g., lives saved, as in the bednet/malaria example).

As for comparing and aggregating impact across multiple grants: A key challenge here is that diverse grants in dissimilar program areas seek different outcomes. Corporate givers who choose to focus high-value grants to just one cause issue are likely to be able to quantify impact in a common natural unit and achieve measurable impact linked back to these grants. For programs such as these, cost-effectiveness analysis is most appropriate. By contrast, cost-benefit analyses assume that grant benefits can be monetized—and therefore the analysis is potentially applicable to aggregating the value of grants applied to many different issues. But cost-benefit analysis makes greater demands on data, funders' assumptions, and value judgments. Funders must collect the data needed to estimate monetary benefits arising from the program and additionally make many subjective judgments about the relative worth of the different social outcomes achieved by different program types. When corporate funders would prefer not to engage on this level (e.g., because they do not have the expertise to collect and calculate the necessary data or make the essential value judgments—or both), the only practical alternative may be to aggregate common output units such as number of activities organized, products distributed, or beneficiaries served.

Figure 5 summarizes this decision framework for guiding the choice of measurement approach. The choice of ROI analysis (if any) to consider depends on the relative focus of the giving programs in question, as well as on the expertise of the funders to calculate and use monetized benefits. The options themselves are discussed in more detail below.

Figure 5: Approaches for Comparing and Aggregating Social Impact Results Across Corporate Grants

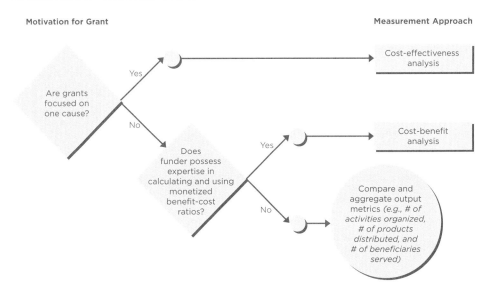

Cost-effectiveness analysis

Cost-effectiveness analysis features the calculation of a ratio of costs (i.e., total contributions to the program) to a non-monetary benefit or outcome. In other words, it indicates a project's "bang for the buck." Program impact is measured in natural units—such as number of children graduated or beneficiaries' life years saved. This comparative analysis requires programs to pursue the same domain area and hence will be more applicable to corporate giving programs that focus fewer high-value grants on a single program area.

One cost-effectiveness approach to calculating ROI is that of the Center for High Impact Philanthropy at the University of Pennsylvania. The Center has been developing its cost-per-impact methodology since 2006. The purpose of its analysis is to provide philanthropists with an answer to the question "How much does change cost?" The example below features a project by the Children's Literacy Initiative (CLI) to train pre-kindergarten through third-grade teachers in effective literacy teaching techniques.

Methodology for University of Pennsylvania Center for High Impact Philanthropy's Cost per Impact

Step 1: Project future cost or take actual cost from previous implementations.

Example: Based on prior experience, CLI estimated that teachers would need three years of training to effect sufficient change and lasting impact. The estimated cost to train twenty teachers for three years is $1,000,000.

Step 2: Obtain empirical results from past implementations of the model and use those to project the impact of current implementation.

Example: Based on national studies and prior experience, the Center and CLI estimated an average kindergarten teacher's tenure to be fourteen years. Since three of those years would be given over to training, the average teacher tenure post-training would be eleven years (14 minus 3). In an evaluation performed in White Plains, NY, 49% of kindergarten students met literacy benchmarks before the CLI training was provided to teachers. Post-training, the proportion increased 32 percentage points to 81%.

Based on an average class size of 25, 25 x 20 teachers = 500 students who would be "touched" by the project each year. Given an average teacher tenure of eleven years, 500 students per year x 11 years = 5,500 students touched. The incremental number of students meeting benchmarks would then be 32% x 5,500 students = 1,760 students.

Step 3: Divide cost obtained in Step 1 by results obtained in Step 2 to produce cost per impact.

Example: Dividing the cost of $1,000,000 by the 1,760 additional students meeting literacy benchmarks yields a cost per incremental student, or cost per impact, of $568.18.

As discussed, one advantage of quantification is that it allows comparison with other projects. Hence, a grantor could use the above cost-per-impact figure to determine which grantee would provide the most "bang for the buck." Alternatively, a grantor could use this figure as a benchmarking tool to identify effective trends and then work with his or her own grantee to improve their own ratio over time.

Source: Rhodes, H. J., Noonan, K., & Rosqueta, K. (December 2008).

Cost-benefit analysis

Cost-benefit analysis is advantageous in that it allows comparison of the social value of diverse programs—much as one can compare the financial ROIs of different companies. Benefits need not come from the same cause and type of outcome but can capture a range of individual and societal benefits across different program areas. However, two recent reviews, by Melinda Tuan (2008) and Lynn Karoly (2008), have noted that the methods for valuing cost-benefits are not yet mature or standardized. Attributing common dollar values to non-monetary results requires subjective value judgments. It is also difficult to achieve consistency in assumptions or applied methodologies, such as (1) the time frame over which benefits are recognized, (2) the discount rate used to reflect the declining value of money over time periods distant in the future, (3) the methods used to project future outcomes based on early outcomes, and (4) the range of social benefits to be captured. Proponents of cost-benefit concepts like the Social Return on Investment (SROI) acknowledge these challenges but also note that the very virtue of cost-benefit analysis lies in human assessors who are brutally open about such subjective valuations and submit assumptions to sensitivity analysis and intuitive assessment. This process can help clarify the extent to which certain projections or judgments are overly optimistic or incomplete.

To consider an example: The Robin Hood Foundation has developed a benefit-cost ratio methodology to capture collective benefit estimates of its anti-poverty grants in four areas: jobs and economic security, education, early childhood, and youth and survival. The benefit-cost ratio seeks to translate the outcome of diverse programs into a single monetized value. The example below features a grant to an organization called Helpful Housing, which provides housing to the economically disadvantaged. Since part of the project involves providing supportive services such as medical care, mental-health counseling, and employment training, the calculation also accounts for those benefits.

Methodology for Robin Hood Foundation Benefit-Cost Ratio

Step 1: Estimate the program's direct impact.

The most direct and tangible benefit provided by Helpful Housing is housing. Therefore, to calculate its value:

Example: Based on data from the Federal Housing and Urban Development Department, Robin Hood found the fair-market prices for New York City apartments to be approximately $11,700 per year. Helpful Housing provided 672 housing units over the last year. It is believed that the people served by Helpful Housing would have remained homeless if Helpful Housing did not exist. Thus, the full market value of the housing provided would represent a net gain to residents. 672 housing units x $11,700 average per year ≈ $7.8 million.

Helpful Housing also provided housing only (i.e., without supportive services) in the form of two-bedroom apartments valued at $13,600 per year to 75 low-income families. Residents are required to contribute only 30% (≈ $2,400) of their annual income toward rent. Robin Hood estimates that 10% of these families would have found housing anyway, even in the absence of Helpful Housing's assistance. So: 75 families x ($13,600 - $2,400) x 0.9 (to account for those families that found housing only as a result of Helpful Housing's assistance) = $760,000.

Step 2: Estimate the additional impact of the program, i.e., benefits from supportive services like medical care, mental-health care, employment training, etc.

It is common for health improvements made by health- and human-service projects to be expressed as Quality-Adjusted Life Years (QALYs), which measure the number of years of life added by an intervention, adjusted for the quality of life in those additional years. By definition, an extra year in perfect health would be assigned a QALY value of 1, while an extra year added in less-than-perfect health would be assigned a QALY value of between 0 and 1, based on the extent of the disability. A commonly accepted guideline proposed by Robin Hood, and used here, is to assume each QALY to be worth $100,000.

Example: *Referrals to Medical Care:* Helpful Housing provided medical referrals to 672 residents. However, it is estimated that 30% of those residents would have sought medical care anyway. External consultants estimate that each medical referral is worth a QALY of 0.07.

672 residents x $100,000 per QALY x 0.07 QALY x 0.7 (to account for the referral) x 0.7 (to account for only those residents who would not have sought medical care were it not for Helpful Housing) ≈ $2.3 million per year.

Similar methodologies were used to calculate other additional annual benefits, such as:

Mental-Health Care ≈ $1.9 million.
Employment Training ≈ $800,000.
Quality-of-Life Issues ≈ $3 million.
Case Management ≈ $2.9 million.
Reduced Hospitalizations and Medical Emergencies ≈ $1.9 million.

Continued

Step 3: Calculate lifetime impact and discount to present value.

Where the benefit is annual and occurs throughout the lifetime of the individual, calculate the cumulative impact over the individual's lifetime and discount to present value.

Example: Robin Hood estimates the average age of residents at Helpful Housing to be 40 years old and calculates employment-related returns to age 55 and health-related returns to age 65. It is assumed that the real growth rate is 3% and the discount rate is 5%. Total Present Value[11] = $31 million.

Step 4: Estimate the proportion of the program's successes truly attributable to Robin Hood's grant (a.k.a. the "Robin Hood factor").

This calculation typically begins with a figure based on the percentage of a grantee's program cost covered by Robin Hood's grant. This approximate starting point is adjusted up or down depending on other factors that lead Robin Hood to believe the grant exerts disproportionate (positive or negative) influence on group outcomes.

Example: Robin Hood's grant was for $450,000; the program cost $12 million in total. That yields a Robin Hood factor of $450,000/$12 million = 4%.

Step 5: Calculate the Robin Hood benefit.

Sum all benefits and scale by the Robin Hood factor.

Example: $31 million x 4% = $2.89 million.

Step 6: Calculate the benefit-cost ratio.

Divide the Robin Hood benefit by the cost of the program.

Example: $2.89 million / $450,000 ≈ 3:1.

Grantors may use this benefit-cost ratio as one important piece of information with which to rank grants (i.e., compare the impact of similar and dissimilar programs) and as part of their diagnostic toolkit, with the goal of improving grantees' performance, thereby raising the projects' benefit-cost ratio over time. However, the ratio should not be the only criterion for making grant decisions, nor should it be used as a report card.

Source: Weinstein, M. (2009).

To translate diverse outcomes into a single, monetized measure of poverty fighting, Robin Hood's program officers rely on social-science research, estimates from academic consultants, close knowledge of their grantees, and an injection of reasonable assumptions. Over time, they expect continually to improve their metrics and reduce guesswork. Additionally, Michael Weinstein (2009), Chief Program Officer of The Robin Hood Foundation, described how the Foundation has addressed a number of other implementation challenges. While benefit-cost ratios provide Robin Hood with a systematic and transparent tool for comparing impact across different program types on its mission, their adoption should not be undertaken except by experts knowledgeable of its careful usage.

Estimating leverage effects

So far, this report has discussed measuring the direct social impact arising from a funder's contribution to a giving program. A funder can also leverage its reputation and/or other non-monetary capabilities to support a program, thereby multiplying the social impact achieved from both their and other funders' monetary donations. These leveraging effects should be considered part of the total merit of a grant or program.

1. Attracting other funders

A funder seen to have expertise in a certain domain could highlight the severity of a social cause by endorsing it and attracting other funders to the same cause. For example, a major pharmaceutical company with a reputation for innovative research might become the first to make significant philanthropic commitments to and educate other funders about the AIDS pandemic in Africa. Evaluating the results achieved by pilot strategies also helps to communicate the credibility and viability of these programs and draw additional support.

2. Capacity building

Grantors can also create social value indirectly by improving the performance of high-potential grantees—maybe by building their operational or leadership structures. Companies can multiply positive effects by contributing internal expertise, technological assistance, and access to training opportunities and other non-cash relationships. For example, enhancing performance-measurement systems provides practical, real-time data that supports learning and allows nonprofits to adjust their services efficiently, thereby maximizing the impact of not just one particular project, but of projects across the entire organization.

> A funder can also leverage its reputation and/or other non-monetary capabilities to support a program, thereby multiplying the social impact achieved from both their and other funders' monetary donations.

Leading users of ROI methodologies consider such leverage effects in their calculations. The Hewlett Foundation estimates the portion of success with which the Foundation could be credited based on a combination of dollar amount invested and the influence of those dollars. The Robin Hood Foundation also estimates similar measures—the Robin Hood factor—as the proportion of program success truly attributable to the giver's intervention. This figure is often based in part (but only in part) on the ratio of the grant to the grantee's total program cost.

Estimating credit for leverage effects requires a combination of subjective judgments and quantitative data. One approach is to reduce this analysis to that of assessing the most likely alternative scenario had the catalytic funder not intervened. Once all subjective and observational inputs have contributed to this hypothetical scenario,[12] the subsequent calculation of leverage effect is straightforward.

Suppose a corporate funder provides a catalytic gift of $2 million towards a health program. The gift raises the program's profile and attracts another $3 million in gifts from other funders, for a total budget of $5 million. This number generates an impact equivalent to 100 QALYs. The corporate funder, through consultations with the grantee and members of the social sector, believes that, without its gift, only $2 million (2/5ths of the actual amount) would have been raised. In this scenario, only 40 (or 2/5ths of the actual 100) QALYs would have been achieved. Therefore, the total impact for which the funder could take credit is the difference: 100 – 40 = 60 QALYs. This number 60 comprises 40 QALYs from direct funding (in proportion to the $2 million grant being 2/5ths of the total budget) and a balance of 20 QALYs credited to the leverage effect.

Consider another example: Suppose a health program with a total budget of $5 million from other funders (i.e., excluding the funder whose leverage is to be measured) delivers 100 QALYs in program impact. Now the leveraging funder can make a capacity-building grant of $1 million, which increases the program's effectiveness such that its impact rises to 150 QALYs. The leveraging funder also estimates (based on consultation with the grantee and other social sector experts) that there would have been only an 80% chance of another capable funder stepping in with a similarly effective capacity-building investment. Thus, the most likely and beneficial alternative scenario is 80% x 150 + (100% - 80%) x 100 = 140 QALYs. The leveraging funder's capacity-building grant can therefore be viewed as achieving 10 QALYs in leverage effects in addition to 23.3 QALYs of direct proportionate impact (because $1 million represents 1/6ths of the total program cost, which delivered 140 total QALYs in the best likely alternative).

Summary

The attractiveness of these ROI methods for calculating corporate philanthropy's social returns is in bringing businesslike, quantitative frameworks to evaluating and comparing the effectiveness of diverse social programs and aggregating their social impact. However, these sophisticated methodologies place heavy demands on data collection, assumptions, and value judgments underlying the analysis. Funders must assemble data and calculations on the program's monetary benefits and make subjective judgments on the relative value of different types of social changes. Corporate funders need to be knowledgeable and thoughtful about these limitations and typically should not rely solely on ROI when evaluating grants. Proponents of these methods note that the benefits of ROI analysis lie more in encouraging funders to lay bare the assumptions and trade-offs that may already be involved in their grantmaking decisions.

Corporate funders who focus their giving on a small number of program areas can define and measure impact using the same natural unit. These results can be analyzed more easily with cost-effectiveness approaches, which sidestep the larger uncertainties associated with cost-benefit analysis and reducing benefits across different program areas to a common monetary unit.

Some ROI models also seek to take into account the leverage benefits the funder may generate if its grant has a catalytic or capacity-building effect. Corporate givers are increasingly committing to capacity-building initiatives, recognizing that the internal expertise, training opportunities, product, and other company resources generate benefits beyond cash grants. Estimating leverage value inevitably requires subjective input. One method for improving a value estimation of leverage is to try to assess and judge what would have resulted from the best likely alternative scenario.

4 For example, The Foundation Center and McKinsey & Company have undertaken a project—an online database of Tools and Resources for Assessing Social Impact (TRASI)—identifying 150 different approaches currently used to measure the social impact of programs. See http://foundationcenter.org/trasi/

5 Motivational categorizations were adapted from the definitions used by London Benchmarking Group (who originated the use of labeling the motivations of corporate giving), the Committee Encouraging Corporate Philanthropy (2009), and the Center on Philanthropy at Indiana University (2007).

6 Kramer & Pfitzer (2007).

7 Kaplan (2002).

8 For example, see the Strive Endorsement Process of Strive Six Sigma, an education partnership based in Cincinnati, Ohio, and Northern Kentucky: http://www.strivetogetherfunders.org/strive_six_sigma

9 Sonal Shah at Social Capital Markets Conference 2009, quoted in Chronicle of Philanthropy Conference Notebook (September 2009). See http://philanthropy.com/news/monthlyconference/2009/09

10 See Charity Navigator's New Course (*Chronicle of Philanthropy*, 2009, July 13).

11 The Present Value of a Growing Annuity is given by $PV = A/(r-g) \times (1-((1+g)/(1+r))T)$, where A = annual benefit, r = discount rate = 5%, g = growth rate = 3%, and T = number of years.

12 This approach shares a similar motivation with the Best Available Charitable Option (BACO) concept used by the Acumen Fund (January 2007) to assess whether the Fund's social investment will outperform a plausible alternative.

CONVERSATION TWO.

Between the Chief Giving Officer (CGO) and Chief Executive Officer (CEO)

According to research by McKinsey and CECP (2008), 86% of surveyed CEOs consider both business and social concerns when funding corporate philanthropy programs—and 55% believe business concerns should be given equal or greater weight than social ones.

When advocating significant commitments to philanthropic initiatives, CGOs are often asked to make a "business case" for those initiatives—to present a persuasive picture of how they create long-term financial value for their companies—in addition to using the social impact-assessment frameworks described above to communicate societal accomplishments.

Question 3.
How to measure business benefits and make a business case?

CEOs surveyed by McKinsey and CECP (2008) cited frequently that corporate philanthropy's business goal should be enhancing the company's reputation or brand, followed by addressing employee concerns such as refining leadership capabilities and building retention and recruitment. The study also reported that efficient philanthropists—defined as respondents who felt their companies were effective in achieving both business and social goals—tended more than other respondents to view the goal of their philanthropic programs as creating business innovation and building new market knowledge.

These findings, combined with a review of the scholarly literature,[13] suggest four strategic pathways by which philanthropic initiatives can contribute to business value:

1. **Enhance employee engagement.** Companies engage employees through group volunteer programs and awareness of their philanthropic initiatives, which raise employee motivation, productivity, and a sense of identification with the organization.

2. **Build customer loyalty.** Especially in consumer-oriented industries, a company's commitment to communities and certain philanthropic causes enhances brand perception, customer loyalty, repeat business, and word-of-mouth promotion.

3. **Manage downside risks to the company's reputation.** Philanthropic initiatives provide companies with a fresh opportunity to prioritize and address stakeholder risks, i.e., ways in which the company may not be meeting public expectations.

4. **Contribute to business innovation and growth opportunities.** Philanthropy also provides access to new relationships and opportunities whereby the company can find, test, and demonstrate new ideas, technologies, and products.

Employee engagement

Today's competitive business environment emphasizes quality and innovation. Accordingly, CEOs recognize that human capital is a more critical asset than physical capital in creating substantial value for the firm and its shareholders. A highly engaged workforce is more likely to exert extra effort and have lower turnover rates. Some studies even show a link between individual employee motivation and company-wide financial performance. Compensation is a motivator only up to a point, beyond which employees are motivated by non-pecuniary factors like self-esteem and recognition. The accepted wisdom seems to be that a paycheck may keep someone on the job physically, but not emotionally. Psychological studies[14] have shown that calling attention to extrinsic (especially monetary) rationales for behavior can diminish performance and intrinsic motivation. Perceiving that they had to be externally and financially induced to carry out a task, employees come to believe that there must not have been any other motivation for performing it. This finding highlights the importance for companies to focus not merely on monetary and other extrinsic rewards alone.

Economists have documented that companies with motivated employees—a category that overlaps considerably with

Fortune Magazine's "100 Best Companies to Work for in America"—enjoy better financial performance. The Best Companies list was first published in a book by Levering, Koskowitz, and Katz in March 1984 and was updated in February 1993. Beginning in 1998, it has been featured in *Fortune* each January. Two-thirds of the total score comes from employee responses to an anonymous, 57-question survey created by the Great Place to Work Institute in San Francisco. The survey provides an extensive evaluation of the level of trust employees have in their management, the level of pride in their work and company, and camaraderie within the workplace. The remaining one-third of the score comes from the Institute's evaluation of factors such as a company's demographic makeup, pay, and benefits packages. Olubunmi Faleye and Emery Trahan (2006), researchers from Northeastern University, examined several dimensions of operating performance and, even after controlling for prior financial performance in their econometric analyses,[15] they found measures of valuation, profitability, and productivity for the Best Companies to be about 15-20% higher than for the Best Companies' peers. Separately, Alex Edmans (2008), a professor of finance at the University of Pennsylvania's Wharton School, found that, on average, the Best Companies achieved higher-than-expected future profits, particularly for earnings far into the future. A portfolio of Best Companies' stocks, based on only prior-released rankings and rebalanced annually, outperformed other similar companies by 4% per year over a 22-year period (from 1984 through 2005). Edmans suggested that because the results of an intangible investment like a motivated workforce may not completely manifest in tangible benefits for several years, the market appears not yet to have fully accounted for the link between employee satisfaction and company value.

To raise employees' internal motivation, HR managers endeavor to improve those employees' sense of status, prestige, belonging within the work group and organization, and emotional rewards inherent in their work. A number of studies have found that corporate philanthropic initiatives can provide a new channel for fulfilling a number of employees' emotional needs and increasing their sense of identification with a company. These initiatives can also help employee recruitment. According to the 2004 corporate community involvement survey by Deloitte LLP, 72% of employed Americans trying to decide between two jobs offering the same location, job description, pay, and benefits would choose to work for the company that also supports charitable causes. Although it is not easy to validate answers to a hypothetical question, companies are often able to document their success in attracting certain top candidates based on those candidates' exposure to the company's philanthropic causes and therefore can claim some legitimate credit for the philanthropy's role in successful recruitment.

A model for measuring the influence of corporate philanthropic initiatives on employee engagement

When devising philanthropic activities for employees, researchers from management and social science disciplines suggest that the key objective companies should target and measure is an increase in an employee's sense of organizational identification. Identification is a psychological concept that (in this context) reflects the extent to which employees feel that their sense of self overlaps with that of their employer. An anecdotal measure of identification is the use of "we" statements by employees who identify strongly with their company—i.e., who have internalized the distinction between "we insiders" and "people outside." C. B. Bhattacharya, Sankar Sen, and Daniel Korschun (2008), researchers from Boston University and Baruch College, found that employees who identify strongly with their company view its success as their own and exhibit higher-performing job behaviors to ensure that success. Caroline Bartel (2001) from New York University and David Jones (2007) from the University of Vermont reported field evaluations whereby they measured both attitudinal and work-behavior changes of employees who participated in their respective company's community-outreach programs. Their research supported the finding that employees involved in philanthropic initiatives showed a statistically significant increase in their sense of identification with their respective companies. This improvement in employee attitudes towards their companies was in turn correlated to an improvement in job performance.

Through awareness of and participation in their employer's philanthropic activities, employees can also fulfill several fundamental emotional needs. The studies noted that the range of emotional needs is quite diverse and companies often do not understand them well:

1. **Collective self-esteem.** Employees want to feel positive about their company and want others to view the company positively as well.

2. **Self-development.** Employees can use philanthropic opportunities both to express a personal sense of community responsibility and to learn specific career-advancement skills. Several major pharmaceuticals and companies in other industries, for example, maintain programs[16] in which top professionals apply their skill sets to work with external nonprofit partners, sometimes in remote foreign locations—and this experience hones those skill sets. (Pfizer[17] has made available an evaluation of the impact of its Global Health Fellows Program on recipient organizations, along with a toolkit that other companies can use to measure their own international corporate volunteering programs.)

3. **Improving work and personal life integration.** Employees interpret employers' philanthropic behavior as an indication that the employer values "personal life" as much as the employee does—particularly when the philanthropy benefits the employee's own social communities.

4. **Building a bridge to the company.** Employees who work in satellite locations view philanthropic initiatives as a means for the company to demonstrate a bond among employees regardless of location. This is especially important as workforces become increasingly globally dispersed.

5. **Creating a "reputation shield."** Corporate philanthropy can help employees combat negative public feedback about a company by giving them material with which to educate external audiences about the company's core values and efforts.

To measure the impact of corporate philanthropy on employee engagement, companies can use internal surveys to assess the extent to which the philanthropic program is meeting employee needs and creating a greater sense of identity between employee and employer. This assessment should take into account the relative importance that different employee segments attach to different intrinsic needs.

Drawing from the research studies reviewed, Figure 6 summarizes the causal relationships between employees' emotional needs and job-related outcomes. Companies able to understand the needs and attitudes of their employees and to design programs that fulfill those needs are often rewarded with greater employee identification and a multitude of other pro-company outcomes.

Figure 6: A Framework for Measuring Employee Engagement and Corporate Philanthropy

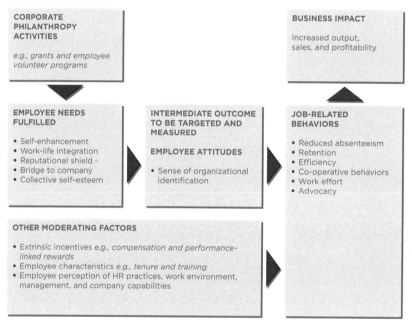

Source: Adapted from Bhattacharya, C. B., Sen, S., & Korschun, D. (2008) and Bartel, C. (2001).

Positive job-related behaviors include objective metrics such as reduced absenteeism, lower employee turnover, and greater efficiency. More subjective outcomes (generally assessed in performance reviews) include enhanced work effort (i.e., greater dedication to excellence and a willingness to expend extra energy), advocacy (i.e., a greater tendency to make suggestions for improvements and innovation), and co-operative conduct.

Conversation between CGO and CEO

Figure 7: Representative Metrics and Survey Instruments from Research Studies in Employee Engagement

Employee Attitude or Job Behavior	References	Metrics and Survey Instruments
Collective self-esteem	Luhtanen & Crocker (1992).	Survey completed by employees with eight-item scale to reflect a member's personal evaluation of the group (private collective self-esteem), as well as his or her assessment of how non-members evaluate the group (public collective self-esteem): 1. I feel good about working for X. 2. I often regret that I work for X. 3. Overall, I often feel that working for X is not worthwhile. 4. In general, I am glad to be an employee of X. 5. Overall, X is considered a good company by others. 6. In general, others respect what X stands for. 7. Most people consider X, on average, to be less effective than other companies. 8. In general, others think that X is not a good company to work for.
Identifies with company	Bagozzi & Bergami (2000), Tropp & Wright (1999).	Survey completed by employees. Survey instrument is a combination of a visual and verbal report in the form of a Venn diagram to assess the degree of cognitive overlap in attributes that an individual uses to define him- or herself and the organization. Employees indicated the pair of overlapping circles that best represented their perceived relationship to the organization (from no overlap to complete overlap). The Venn diagram is supplemented with a second item that asked members to report the degree of overlap between their self-image and their image of the organization.
Retention	Phillips (2005).	(Voluntary) Turnover (%).
Absenteeism	Phillips (2005).	Days absent per year.
Efficiency	Phillips (2005).	Sales per employee.
Co-operative behaviors	McAllister (1995).	Survey completed by managers with ten-item scale to reflect affiliation, co-operation, and assistant co-operation behaviors: 1. Takes time to listen to other people's problems and worries. 2. Rarely takes a personal interest in others. 3. Frequently does something extra that won't be rewarded, but which makes co-operative efforts with others more productive. 4. Passes on information that might be useful to others. 5. Willingly helps others, even at some cost to personal productivity. 6. Rarely takes others' needs/feelings into account when making decisions that affect others. 7. Tries not to make things more difficult for others at work. *continued*

Figure 7: Representative Metrics and Survey Instruments from Research Studies in Employee Engagement, *continued*

Employee Attitude or Job Behavior	References	Metrics and Survey Instruments
		8. Goes out of his/her way to help co-workers with difficult assignments. 9. Offers to help others who have heavy workloads. 10. Covers for absent co-workers.
Work effort	Van Dyne, Graham, & Dienesch (1994).	Survey completed by managers with ten-item scale to measure work effort and willingness to expend energy on the organization's behalf: 1. Rarely wastes time while at work. 2. Produces as much as is capable of at all times. 3. Always comes to work on time. 4. Regardless of circumstances, produces highest-quality work. 5. Does not meet all departmental deadlines. 6. Is mentally alert and ready to work when he/she arrives at work. 7. Follows work rules and instructions with extreme care. 8. Sometimes wastes departmental resources. 9. Keeps work area clean and neat. 10. Sometimes misses work for no good reason.
Advocacy participation	Van Dyne, Graham, & Dienesch (1994).	Survey completed by managers with seven-item scale to assess advocacy participation behaviors indicative of innovation, maintaining high standards, and making suggestions for change: 1. Uses personal judgment to assess what might be right/wrong for the department. 2. Encourages management and co-workers to keep knowledge and skills current. 3. Encourages others to speak up and participate in meetings. 4. Does not push co-workers to establish higher standards at work. 5. Keeps self well-informed where his/her opinion might matter. 6. Helps co-workers think for themselves. 7. Frequently gives co-workers creative suggestions for ways of accomplishing tasks.

Figure 7 lists the metrics and survey instruments (whereby respondents are asked to score on a numerical scale) used in representative studies.

Bartel's (2001) study posed survey questions to employees and their supervisors both before and after the employees participated in the company's community-outreach program. To form a control group, supervisors were also asked to evaluate a group of non-participants. Comparing differences in pre- and post-program survey reports, Bartel found that participation enhanced the collective self-esteem of employees. In turn, those employees also perceived a statistically stronger level of identification with the company. For employees whose organizational identification became stronger, their supervisors reported higher interpersonal co-operation and work-related effort—whereas the supervisors reported no statistically significant changes in any work behavior by the control group. Bartel also measured and controlled for other factors that might have influenced her results, such as employee characteristics like length of tenure, prior community-outreach experience, and job responsibilities.

To quantify the financial value of improved employee behavior, one can estimate a statistical regression model of how much employees' organizational identification correlated to productivity value. The underlying data supporting such analysis needs to come from linking employee survey results to HR data such as performance reviews and productivity metrics. Relative employee-performance rankings, efficiency, attendance, retention, and other employee attributes then must be translated to relative dollar values.[18] To improve the model's statistical validity and to justify this performance proxy, other control variables must be accounted for, such as job definition, location, training, age, and company tenure. Given the overlap of this analysis with broader HR evaluations, it is sensible to integrate this exercise into HR's systematic procedures. Designing and implementing a centralized form of measurement reduces survey fatigue and ensures the consistency and comprehensiveness of surveys' data and approach. Figure 8 outlines how, once a general model is built and calibrated, financial returns can be estimated by applying the model to employees' survey scores. Researchers in HR management[19] have noted that many senior company managers may be more pragmatic about what HR evaluation can measure and do not need to quantify the financial benefit from HR programs; they believe it is

Figure 8: Model to Estimate the Influential Value of Corporate Philanthropic Initiatives on Employee Productivity

Measure increase in level of employees' identification with company *e.g., analysis of pre- and post-activity surveys*	**X**	Estimate dollar value of increase in productivity from employees with greater identification with company *e.g., estimate regression model statistically from study where data from employee surveys have been linked to performance ratings and productivity metrics*	**=**	Estimated value of employee productivity

sufficient to measure that individual employees' motivational needs are met and their emotional attitudes towards the organization improved.

Customer loyalty

Marketing managers have long recognized that securing customer loyalty is a valuable goal, partly because retaining customers tends to require fewer marketing resources than recruiting new ones. Moreover, customer loyalty consistently shows high correlation to sales growth and profitability. Loyal customers demonstrate several pro-company behaviors: they tend to re-purchase the company's product or service, commit a higher share of their category spending to the company, and are more likely to recommend the company or brand to new customers.[20] Traditional marketing strategies often focus on customer-loyalty scores and on improving loyalty by enhancing customers' perceptions of the product's quality and value. The perception of a company's values through its philanthropic programs also matters, of course. All else being equal, a consumer is more likely to choose a product made by a highly responsible company than one made by a less responsible one.

Geoffrey Heal (2008) of Columbia Business School recounted the customer-research experience of a consumer goods company. The company had built a customer-loyalty model based on a composite of its customers' responses to seven survey instruments: whether they (1) ask for the brand, (2) re-purchase the same brand, (3) recommend the brand, (4) use other products by the same brand, (5) overrule a salesperson pushing another brand, (6) will only buy the brand, and/or (7) switch stores for the brand. "Passionately loyal" customers are defined as those who answer affirmatively to at least four of those seven questions. The company estimated that a one-percentage point increase in their brand's Customer Loyalty Index (CLI)—the percentage of all customers who are passionately loyal—translated into a nearly 5% increase in sales. Furthermore, the company's research revealed that its customers' emotional motivations were twice as important as product considerations in driving brand loyalty. Out of about fifty touch-points tested, social responsibility was among the top five important factors to consumers in terms of loyalty. Accordingly, the company learned that it could increase its emotional connection with consumers by tying its brand to the company's commitment to a social cause.

A model for measuring the influence of corporate philanthropy initiatives on customer loyalty

Customer-loyalty scores are typically measured by surveys that ask consumers to rank their intentions to re-purchase or recommend a product according to a numerical scale. Measuring customer intentions rather than actual purchasing behaviors provides companies with a more timely and operable loyalty assessment. Researchers may implement different proxies, however—ranging from a composite survey that measures multiple customer intentions to a single best metric like the Net Promoter Score,[21] which is based on customers' intention to re-purchase. Companies periodically validate intentions by following up on customers' actual behaviors. This more-involved validation exercise also allows the company to calibrate how much sales growth can be expected as a result of increased loyalty.

Because marketing managers have traditionally focused on product or service performance as drivers for customer loyalty, the attention has long been on customer satisfaction and trust in the brand. But customer awareness of a company's philanthropic efforts is an additional channel by which loyalty can be achieved. Presenting the findings of a telephone survey conducted among a national sample of 1,033 adults, the 2004 Cone Corporate

> ...a company's philanthropic involvement can lead customers to feel a deeper sense of identification with the company and develop a more positive evaluation of the company's abilities...

Citizenship Study reported that eight in ten Americans agree that corporate support of a cause wins their trust. Moreover, 86% said that if the quality and price of a product are equal, they would be likely to switch brands in order to help support a cause. Field research studies have shown that a company's philanthropic involvement can lead customers to feel a deeper sense of identification with the company and develop a more positive evaluation of the company's abilities—and that this results in product purchases. However, these studies have also found and emphasized that the pathway from customer awareness of corporate philanthropy to loyalty is less straightforward than hypothetical marketplace polls and surveys suggest. Victoria Smith and Peter Langford (2009) from Macquarie University in Australia and C. B. Bhattacharya and Sankar Sen (2004) from Boston University and Baruch College document that customers' perceptions and expectations can be complex when confronted with a company's corporate philanthropic record—and suggest that this affects how much philanthropic initiatives actually do translate into increased loyalty and purchases:

- Consumers' lack of awareness about philanthropic initiatives is often a major limiting factor in their ability to respond. At the same time, disingenuous attempts by the company to "sell" philanthropy can backfire.

- Philanthropic initiatives are more likely to lead to positive customer behaviors when the cause is perceived to fit well within a company's overall strategy.

- Consumers view companies that base their business strategies around socially responsible principles more positively than companies that attempt social responsibility as an add-on action.

- Consumers may be skeptical when a company with a negative reputation becomes involved in causes closely related to its business.

- Different personality traits result in different responses to corporate philanthropy efforts: what works for one consumer segment may not work for another. Individuals who personally support the issue central to the company's initiatives are more likely to be persuaded to purchase its products. Companies perceived to have distinguished themselves on a corporate-responsibility platform generally enjoy a loyal following among a certain segment of customers.

- Consumers generally do not like to be asked to pay a premium for philanthropy, nor do they want to sacrifice product quality.

- Perception of a company's capabilities in other areas also modifies how consumers respond to philanthropy. Researchers have identified a strong statistical relationship between consumer satisfaction and companies' philanthropic record *only* when companies are perceived to have strong product quality and innovation capabilities and/or operate in consumer-oriented industries.[22]

Designing a measurement framework for loyalty should begin with an assessment of the perceptions customers have already developed as a result of a company's corporate philanthropic initiatives—and whether these perceptions are contributing to higher loyalty scores. Figure 9 suggests such a framework, based on the literature reviewed.

Figure 9: A Framework for Measuring Customer Loyalty and Corporate Philanthropy

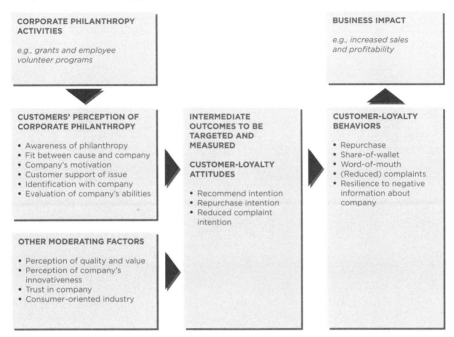

Source: Adapted from Bhattacharya, C.B., Sen, S. (2004), and Smith, V., & Langford, P. (2009).

A company's marketing department is likely already to have implemented its own customer loyalty metrics, in which case it is sensible to leverage these along with customized, deliberate customer research. It is imperative that the additional factors affecting loyalty scores—e.g., customer perceptions of product quality and value—also be taken into account. Figure 10 proposes representative survey instruments that companies may adapt.

Figure 10: Representative Metrics and Survey Instruments from
Research Studies in Customer Loyalty

Customer Perceptions	References	Metrics and Survey Instruments
Fit between company and philanthropic initiatives	Becker-Olsen & Hill (2005).	Survey with four-item scale: 1. There is a low/strong fit between the company and philanthropic initiative. 2. There is dissimilarity/similarity between company and philanthropic initiative. 3. There is inconsistency/consistency between company and philanthropic initiative. 4. The company and philanthropic initiative are complementary/not complementary.
Company's motivation is intrinsic (socially motivated)	Du, Bhattacharya, & Sen (2007).	The company supports this philanthropic initiative because it is genuinely concerned about being socially responsible.
Company's motivation is extrinsic (profit-motivated)	Du, Bhattacharya, & Sen (2007).	The company supports this philanthropic initiative because it feels competitive pressures to engage in such activities.
Beliefs about company's social responsibility	Du, Bhattacharya, & Sen (2007).	1. This company/brand is a socially responsible company/brand. 2. This company/brand has made a real difference through its socially responsible actions.
Customer identification with company	Becker-Olsen & Hill (2005).	My sense of who I am (i.e., my personal identity) overlaps with my sense of what this company represents.
Customer loyalty: intention to re-purchase	Bone & Ellen (1992).	Survey with three-item scale assessing customers' intention to purchase: 1. What is the probability that you will use X's services? 2. What is the likelihood of you choosing X the next time you contract a service? 3. The next time I purchase a service will be with X.
Customer loyalty: intention to recommend	Reichheld (2003).	How likely is it that you would recommend X to a friend or colleague?

CEOs have a keen interest in quantifying the financial value of loyal customers. A statistical model of the expected lifetime value of customer loyalty—reflecting the profits likely to arise from re-purchases and word-of-mouth recommendations—is a helpful indicator as to the returns from loyalty-enhancement. Attributions of customer loyalty can be further broken down: statistical techniques such as "conjoint analysis"[23] can be applied to customer surveys to assess how much a customer's perception of corporate philanthropy contributed to his or her loyalty score. Figure 11 outlines how companies can then estimate financial returns from corporate philanthropy's influence on customer loyalty.

Figure 11: Model to Estimate the Influential Value of Corporate Philanthropic Initiatives on Customer Loyalty

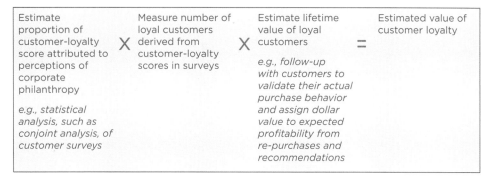

| Estimate proportion of customer-loyalty score attributed to perceptions of corporate philanthropy *e.g., statistical analysis, such as conjoint analysis, of customer surveys* | X | Measure number of loyal customers derived from customer-loyalty scores in surveys | X | Estimate lifetime value of loyal customers *e.g., follow-up with customers to validate their actual purchase behavior and assign dollar value to expected profitability from re-purchases and recommendations* | = | Estimated value of customer loyalty |

Managing reputational risk

A strong and positive reputation is invaluable to a company. How external stakeholders see a company as "good" rather than "bad" reinforces the company with better human capital, goodwill, legitimacy, and a license to operate in the communities it serves and seeks to enter. However, as Benjamin Franklin once said, "it takes many good deeds to build a good reputation and only one bad one to lose it."

Managing downside reputational risk before a crisis strikes is critical; much less can be done after the crisis has occurred. Researchers have documented how a record of community-based initiatives creates goodwill that can mitigate stakeholder sanctions ranging from mild (e.g., casual bad-mouthing) to severe (having one's right to do business revoked) when negative events arise.

Paul Godfrey, Craig Merrill, and Jared Hansen (2009) of Brigham Young University point out that the severity of such sanctions may depend on both the negative effects of the action and the perceived intentions of the offending company. In other words: punishments are more severe when "bad acts are committed by bad actors." Moreover, long-accumulated goodwill, trust, and familiarity can moderate the negative reputational effect of a company blunder, as these traits often encourage stakeholders to attribute the negative event to a singular managerial mistake rather than an intentional course.

To test this idea, Godfrey, Merrill, and Hansen collected and examined stock-price reactions for a large sample of companies that experienced negative legal or regulatory actions. Such negative events, to the extent that they are unanticipated or partially anticipated, should generate negative stock-price

> ...long-accumulated goodwill, trust, and familiarity can moderate the negative reputational effect of a company blunder...

reactions as investors expect negative stakeholder reactions. However, commitment to community initiatives could serve as a signal to investors of the goodwill and positive perception of management character enjoyed by the company and which may temper possible sanctions. The researchers examined 160 companies that appeared from 1991 to 2002 in a dataset maintained by the research firm KLD Analytics. The dataset contains analysts' assessments of the companies' social participation in community and diversity initiatives. The researchers also reviewed *Wall Street Journal* articles published between 1992 and 2003, looking for negative events such as the initiation of a lawsuit against any of the companies by a customer, third party, or competitor; or the announcement of regulatory action (e.g., investigation, fines, penalties, etc.) by a government entity. The announcement events were grouped into either "integrity-based" actions such as discrimination claims, fraud accusations, false claims/dishonesty, pension or investor obligation claims, or bribery allegation; and "competitive or health/safety" actions including competition conspiracy, anti-trust claims, patent infringements, price-fixing accusations, consumer medical/injury issues, product-safety problems, quality-control issues, and environmental/pollution indiscretions. The researchers reported that companies participating in social initiatives preserved greater share value (adjusted for market-wide price movement) around these negative announcements than those who did not participate in social initiatives. However, the data does not reveal the relative severity of the negative events; hence the study was unable to control for the possibility that the missteps done by "good" companies simply were not as "bad" as those done by the companies less socially engaged. The value effects were strongest surrounding those events categorized as "integrity-related." In a back-of-the-envelope calculation, the researchers estimated that companies not engaging in social initiatives lost, on average, $72.4 million per negative event, while socially engaged companies lost only $22.8 million (relative to the average market capitalization of $32.6 billion for all companies on the days preceding the events).

A model for measuring the value of corporate philanthropy in terms of managing reputational risk

Many companies already have in place a strategy for managing reputational risk. This strategy typically includes identifying events that may lead to reputational damage, assessing the likelihood and severity of damage, and preparing plans to manage these risks.[24] The first step in assessing these risks is to identify key stakeholders (internal and external, such as customers, suppliers, and regulators), understand their expectations vis-à-vis the company's current reputation, and develop a master list of risk events. A starting point for identifying reputational threats is a list of stakeholder groups and their corresponding threats—as analyzed by Charles Fombrun, Naomi Gardberg, and Michael Barnett (2000) of New York University and summarized in Figure 12. To quantify stakeholder expectations and reputational risks, a company's Enterprise Risk Management or Public Relations department may conduct a reputation assessment, often applying one or more of the following techniques: (1) analysis of media hits and stories, (2) interviews with front-line employees, (3) consultations with stakeholders and industry executives, (4) focus groups, and (5) public opinion polls.[25]

Precise valuation of reputational insurance against these threats is difficult. When litigation, community protests, and other crises are successfully avoided, costs will never be recorded and the resulting impact on profits or share prices goes unobserved. However, these costs can be real and significant. Scenario analysis is a tool commonly used in addressing such problems and estimating the potential cost of these risks. Each potential event needs to be assessed in terms of the likelihood that it will occur and the severity of the potential reputational damage, as suggested in Figure 13. Companies can perform a quantitative assessment of the impact of reputational damage in terms of reduced operating revenue or increased compliance, operating, or capital costs. This may involve simulation techniques to map out numerous scenarios and estimate average frequency and loss severity. The company can then prioritize these risks and decide whether and how they can be eliminated, reduced, or accepted.

Figure 12: Identifying Stakeholder Groups and Reputational Threats

Stakeholder	Threats	Examples
Community	Withdraw license to operate	Companies seek to dampen community protests and threats to the legitimacy of their operations.
Regulators	Regulatory action	Companies seek to create greater trust and familiarity between themselves and the local community and regulators, reducing the likelihood and costs of regulatory actions.
Customers	Misunderstanding	Companies want to convey favorable images of themselves and reduce the chance that customers misunderstand their business behavior and ethics.
Partners	Defection	Companies want to reduce the risks of disruption to crucial flows of manufacturing inputs, products, services, and resources.
Employees	Rogue behavior	Companies want to strengthen the bond between employees and the corporate culture and avoid actions taken by employees in their self-interest that can create negative publicity for a company or even bring it down.
Investors	Share value	Companies want to assure investors of their future prospects for growth, stability of profitability, and quality of management.
Activists	Boycotts	Companies are more vulnerable to activists if their actions, or inactions, can be perceived as damaging to social values or communities.
Media	Negative exposure	When a crisis arises, a company can be vulnerable to negative media exposure both if the company is too quiet or too vocal/visible. The company can reduce this vulnerability by nurturing a positive corporate image and appropriately familiarizing the public with its business, employees, and activities.

Source: Adapted from Fombrun, C. J., Gardberg, N. A., & Barnett, M. L. (2000).

Figure 13: Quantitative Assessment of Reputational Risk Events: Regulatory Action Example

Risk	Cost Types	Costs	X	Likelihood	=	Expected Loss
Legislative adjustments that change the rules of the game	• Lost revenues • Increased taxes and tariffs	$........ $........		........%		$........

Source: Adapted from Epstein, M. J. (2008), Figure 7.3.

Conversation between CGO and CEO

Positioning corporate philanthropy either internally or externally is not straightforward. Companies need to be wary that stakeholders might cynically perceive these initiatives as just empty claims or public relation devices. Corporate philanthropy needs to represent and be embedded in a natural extension of the company's values and operations. NGOs and nonprofit partners who speak on companies' behalf bring more credibility. At the same time, the bigger a company's reputation and the larger the gap between perception and reality, the more vulnerable the company is to reputational attacks.

Innovation and growth opportunities

Innovation, which is key to sustaining a competitive business advantage, often emerges from creative problem solving. Rosabeth Moss Kanter (1999) of Harvard Business School has suggested that companies can view community need as a business opportunity—to develop ideas, demonstrate technologies, find and serve new markets, and solve longstanding social problems. Companies can further their capabilities by applying their best people and core skills to advancement that benefits both business and community. Kanter even goes so far as to suggest thinking about these efforts not simply as charity but as "a strategic business investment." Jane Nelson and Beth Jenkins (2006) of Harvard University reviewed several examples of companies "looking to their philanthropic, community investment and employee volunteering programs as sources of innovation for the company, its partners, and the communities and countries in which it operates."

Sarah Holmes and Lance Noir (2007), from Cranfield University in the U.K., studied innovation's role in companies' collaborative relationships with nonprofit organizations. As drivers of innovation disperse beyond traditional company boundaries, access to a diverse range of external partners becomes increasingly valuable to companies wishing to generate and be associated with new ideas. Nonprofits offer companies access to a dense network distinct from the companies' own corporate sphere—as well as a fresh view of the modern marketplace. NGOs, for example, lead social movements and can give early

> ...access to a diverse range of external partners becomes increasingly valuable to companies wishing to generate and be associated with new ideas.

warning about shifts in public tastes and values. They may also possess unique technical expertise and influence on public legislation, resources that corporate partners are likely to find advantageous when exploring new markets.

As suggested by a Boston College Center for Corporate Citizenship and McKinsey & Company (2009) review of practices among twenty companies, philanthropic activities could have a demonstrable impact on corporate growth through several "pathways":

- **New markets.** Philanthropic activities expose companies to new markets and increase market share through exposure.

- **New products.** Philanthropic activities can involve the creation of products that meet social needs and increase differentiation.

- **New customers.** Philanthropic activities engage new and existing consumers and contribute to a greater understanding of consumer expectations and behavior.

- **New technologies.** Philanthropic activities can lead to the development of cutting-edge technologies and innovative products also applicable to business use, patenting, and proprietary knowledge.

The financial impact arising from these philanthropic activities ranges from profits increased directly, through sales, or indirectly, through goodwill or savings related to risk avoidance or operating-efficiency gains.

Models for measuring the value of corporate philanthropy in terms of innovation and growth opportunities

There are three standard financial valuation methods that can be applied to measure the value of corporate philanthropy as an opportunity for business innovation and growth:

I. Market-based model

The market-based approach is the most straightforward. It relies, however, on being able either to observe a market price for the project in question or comparisons to the market values of other similar projects or assets. For example, innovation may result in a new patent, which has a market price when put up for sale to other companies. Another example: if other similar businesses already have a market price, then the project can be valued by applying the same financial multiples—e.g., price-to-book value or price-to-earnings ratios—of those comparables.

II. Cash-flow model

The income- or cash flow-based approach is often used instead of the market-based model because market prices are not readily available, particularly for unique projects or projects that cannot easily be isolated and assessed as stand-alone entities. All future cash flows are estimated and then discounted to arrive at their net present value. The three steps comprising the cash flow-based approach are:

1. Estimate future cash flows, including revenues and expenses. This captures the enhanced revenues or savings the innovation has effected.

2. Determine the time period over which these cash flows are earned.

3. Apply an appropriate discount rate, which reflects the time-value of money and the relative risk or uncertainty of cash flows.

III. Real-options analysis model

Innovations can also provide companies with the potential to create cash flows that will exist in the future but do not exist now. For example, a company may develop a new commercial technology as a residual benefit from sustained efforts tackling a social-sector objective. This technology may not be financially viable today, which is why the company does not commercialize it and does not enjoy any current cash flow owing to its existence. Nevertheless, the technology may have considerable value to the company because it can be developed in the future. Financial scholars including Aswath Damodaran (2006) have noted that such examples of intangible assets may be undervalued on a traditional cash-flow basis and are best valued using the real-options approach. Charles Fombrun and his co-researchers (2000) have also suggested that, "were firms to view citizenship through the real-options lens, they might overcome these myopic tendencies [to under-invest in it]."

To illustrate the valuation concepts underlying the real-options approach, consider a hypothetical example of a company gaining access to a new market[26] through exposure from its philanthropic programs. Small-medium-sized enterprises (SMEs) in an emerging market country can form a sizable customer base for their products. However, start-up costs for a business venture are substantial and business revenues, though potentially large, are still highly uncertain. So an established company funds a philanthropic initiative that helps SME owners to develop their business knowledge and capabilities. This initiative not only improves the company's access to potential customers, but over time also allows it to develop and gauge market opportunities for its commercial products. The company can choose to enter the market itself if and when it is determined financially viable—or it may choose not to, in which case it has protected its downside financial risk, all the while contributing to improving socio-economic conditions.

In practice, calculating real-options values requires sophisticated numerical techniques and should be undertaken with business units in the firm, to ensure consistent assumptions are used. Nevertheless, its intuition can be illustrated by adding some numbers to this stylized example. Assume a company's cost of capital is 10%. Start-up costs in a new market are $60 million, while market size may be drawn from three equally likely scenarios: annual revenue streams of $3 million, $6 million, or $12 million. Using the cash flow-based approach, the expected (i.e., probability-weighted average) discounted value of these perpetual revenue streams is $70 million. Therefore, the net present value, subtracting start-up costs, is $10 million.

However, suppose the company is able to narrow this uncertainty after engaging in those philanthropic initiatives. The company would decide to go ahead only if it knew that the market presented the highest-revenue scenario, where the company would likely earn $120 million - $60 million = $60 million. The discounted probability-weighted average profits would be (1 - 10%) x (1/3 x $60 million) = $18 million, since one would not proceed in the other two cases.

Only the real-options approach allows a company the flexibility to wait and see if commercialization is viable. This flexibility can protect downside risk and is financially most valuable to the company when:

1. There is greater uncertainty about the size of the market.

2. There is substantial investment needed for infrastructure.

3. There are significant barriers to entry for competitors. Even when a leading company cannot keep competitors completely at bay (unlike with a patent protected by law), it can still reap a disproportionate share of benefits by being the first to build a superior reputation and relationships in the new market.

Summary

CGOs can make a more persuasive business case by articulating clearly the strategies by which they expect philanthropic initiatives to contribute towards strategic business needs, such as improved employee engagement, customer loyalty, reputational risk, and growth opportunities. These pathways are often not straightforward. To realize meaningful benefits, philanthropic involvement cannot be treated as just another "check in the box." Companies must understand the mechanisms by which they expect these business benefits to be achieved. Related business disciplines have developed a body of evidence and measurement approaches that can be applied. When benefits to the business are long-term or intangible, modeling approaches for valuing future cash flows, analyzing scenarios, and calibrating expected monetary profits linked to the behaviors of loyal customers and engaged employees can be used to estimate financial value as well as to clarify assumptions. Intermediate metrics can help programs deliver those business benefits by enabling managers to make mid-course adjustments as necessary.

Companies who find natural, innovative opportunities to commit a broad array of company product, expertise, and capabilities beyond cash grants can multiply the business and social returns that their philanthropic initiatives achieve. These opportunities are more likely to arise when companies establish meaningful, long-term relationships with nonprofit partners aligned with the company's priority areas. When corporate donations are disbursed without strategy, the benefits will be greatly limited.

Heike Bruch and Frank Walter (2005), from the University of St. Gallen in Switzerland, distinguish companies as being market- or competence-oriented in their philanthropic focus. Endeavoring to live up to stakeholder expectations, these market-oriented companies are likely to care most about measuring competitive advantages such as improved marketing capabilities and better stakeholder relationships. By contrast, competence-oriented companies focus on internal skills when deciding on the nature of their charitable involvement—and, for such companies, measuring value from employee engagement and business innovation is more important than for market-oriented

> When corporate donations are disbursed without strategy, the benefits will be greatly limited.

companies. The best approach would seem to be a balanced combination: of an external (market) *and* internal (competence) orientation—which would be more likely to maximize business and social benefits concurrently.

---

13 This review focused on studies that concentrated on companies' social and community behavior, which for many companies begins with corporate philanthropy: the charitable donation of dollars, products, services, and employee volunteer time. Some of these studies also considered a company's broader corporate citizenship performance, beyond social and community engagement, and included other aspects of corporate social responsibility (CSR), such as governance structure and environmental impact.

14 Known in the psychology literature as the motivation-crowding theory. See Frey & Jegen (2001) and Weibel, Rost, & Osterloh (2007).

15 A recurring statistical criticism of such empirical studies is: How can one disentangle the possibility that companies for whom employees enjoy working might simply be financially valuable in the first place? Researchers attempt to mitigate this problem by including in their regression models a slew of control variables, such as measures of past financial performance. More rigorous statistical tests require controlled experiments and field studies that are more complex to undertake.

16 Hills & Mahmud (2007).

17 See http://www.pfizer.com/responsibility/global_health/global_health_fellows.jsp

18 One can turn to the HR measurement field for calculation and estimation approaches to convert outcomes from an HR program to monetary values, although no standard approach exists. For example, Phillips (2005) provides a review of HR measurement strategies and describes (pp. 182-183) how a large financial institution, RBS, developed and used an employee-engagement model to link HR information to key business indicators, enabling the business to measure the impact of HR initiatives on business profits.

19 In a survey of HR managers and corporate executives who sponsor executive education programs, Charlton & Osterweil (2005) found that while respondents agreed that measuring ROI was important, people may mean different things when they talk about ROI. The researchers conclude that "sponsors may not be as wedded to proof of financial ROI as many HR professionals assume."

20 Reichheld & Sasser (1990).

21 Reichheld (2003).

22 Luo & Bhattacharya (2006) and Lev, Petrovits, & Radhakrishnan (2009).

23 Conjoint analysis is a statistical technique that originated in mathematical psychology and is applied to marketing and survey analyses. See Green & Srinivasan (1990). The technique uses statistical decompositional methods to quantify consumers' relative preferences given their overall evaluations of a set of alternatives, which in turn are specified as levels of different attributes.

24 Christiaens (2008).

25 Eccles, Newquist, & Schatz (2007).

26 To illustrate the potential role of philanthropic programs, this hypothetical example was adapted from the field of international business management. For example, Li & Rugman (2007) investigated how to apply real-options analysis to foreign direct investment decisions made by multinational enterprises. The focus of their paper was on only traditional market-entry modes such as exports, licensing, and wholly owned subsidiaries.

Conversation between CGO and CEO

CONVERSATION THREE.
Between the Chief Executive Officer (CEO) and investor community

The investor community tends to pose two contrasting questions about corporate giving. On the one hand, shareholders want assurance that philanthropy adds to or at least does not detract from shareholder value. On the other hand, a growing number of investors place increasing emphasis on the demonstration of corporate responsibility. A large body of literature already exists seeking to demonstrate the business value of corporate philanthropy to both groups. Merely for ease of distinction here, we will distinguish these two investor groups as "traditional" and "responsible."

Question 4.
How to measure the value of corporate philanthropy for traditional investors?

Scholars have long searched for a link between corporate philanthropy and premiums in company profits or stock prices. They believe that if this link can be proven statistically, it could offer definitive financial justification for companies to behave as good corporate citizens. Textbook accounting frameworks reveal that a company's share-price multiple—the premium that a company's share price may be worth over its book value of identifiable company assets—can be driven higher through two financial levers[27]: (1) a lower cost of capital, or (2) higher expectations of how much future profitability exceeds the company's cost of capital. The share-price premium that a company enjoys over its cost of identifiable financial and physical assets is attributed to intangibles, which can comprise a significant portion of a company's intrinsic value.[28]

Empirical evidence on share-price valuations and profitability

Baruch Lev and Christine Petrovits at New York University and Suresh Radhakrishnan (2009) at the University of Texas collected a large dataset of charitable contributions made by public companies from 1989 through 2000. They applied a statistical methodology known as Granger causality, which distinguishes causation from association, and found that charitable contributions increased the subsequent revenue growth of their donors. This causal relationship was found only in industries highly sensitive to consumer perception—and for these consumer-oriented companies within their sample period, a basic calculation suggests that giving $500,000 caused net profits to rise by almost $800,000. The researchers could not detect a relationship between charitable giving and profits (nor sales growth) in non-consumer industries such as industrial companies.

A study by Ray Fisman and Geoffrey Heal of Columbia Business School and Vinay Nair (2007) of the Wharton School used a different dataset to explore similar hypotheses. They collected financial data from 1991 to 2003 to calculate profitability and price-to-book ratios for individual companies and also collected information about average advertising intensity for different industries. Philanthropy ratings came from the SOCRATES database maintained by KLD Research and Analytics. Similarly to Lev et al, these researchers found a positive statistical relationship between philanthropy and company financial performance as measured by profitability and price-to-book ratios only in advertising-intensive industries, such as consumer-oriented companies. However, the economic magnitude detected was not large.

Joshua Margolis, Hillary Elfenbein, and James Walsh (2007), from Harvard Business School, University of California and University of Michigan, respectively, conducted a review of 167 similar scholarly studies. They concluded that, after thirty-five years of research, the preponderance of scholarly evidence suggests a mildly positive relationship between corporate social performance and corporate financial performance and finds no indication that corporate social investments systematically decrease shareholder value.[29] More critically, they and other researchers have acknowledged a number of weaknesses in the methodologies and data comprising these studies. Even when such economic links exist, flaws such as these would reduce the power of statistical tests to prove them:

> ...the preponderance of scholarly evidence suggests a mildly positive relationship between corporate social performance and corporate financial performance and finds no indication that corporate social investments systematically decrease shareholder value.

1. There is wide variation in how companies are assessed on their corporate social performance. Many studies use observer perceptions or insiders' self-reported impressions that may suffer from biases (e.g., the "halo effect"). Others use third-party audits that are often not transparent or open to validation. Simple metrics like contribution amounts do not reflect how effectively donation dollars are actually spent.

2. Much of the business value of corporate philanthropy can be classified as contributing to the "intangibles" of a company, which may only show up in profits several years later—and many studies do not examine the impact on profits over a sufficiently long time frame. There is also mixed evidence on how efficiently stock markets price companies whose intangibles make up a large proportion of their value.

3. Some studies measure financial performance as positive market-adjusted stock-price returns. These results can be sensitive to the sample period chosen. Ideally, a study would observe a long period that effectively smoothes out the high variability in stock-price movement and spans full economic cycles. Even more critically, care must be taken when interpreting the hypotheses supported by such tests. If philanthropic companies are successful in attracting more investors and raising capital at a lower cost, one would expect the stock-price multiples of these companies to be higher and average stock returns *lower* than for less philanthropic companies. When stocks are priced efficiently, the lower cost of capital required by investors in philanthropic companies should match the lower average returns they subsequently earn over time as a result of holding those stocks. Research by Harrison Hong and Marcin Kacperczyk (2007), from Princeton University and the University of British Columbia,

respectively, illustrates such a relationship with tobacco companies. To date, the tobacco industry represents the most prevalent negative-screen applied by socially responsible investors. Over the past three and a half decades, tobacco stocks, consistent with losing access to capital from a class of investors,[30] have been priced at lower multiples: their price-to-book multiples were 15% lower than non-tobacco stocks. At the same time, consistent with having to deliver a higher return on capital, average stock returns from these "sin" stocks outperformed other comparable stocks by approximately 2-4% a year.

4. Many studies are inexplicit about the direction of causality. Can companies afford to be more philanthropic because they have performed better financially, rather than the other way around? Studies also must control for other company characteristics that drive financial performance but may be correlated to philanthropic spending—such as industry, risk, size, research and development, and advertising expenditures.

5. Across companies, the relationship between corporate philanthropy and financial performance is quite complex. Researchers[31] have found the relationship to be nonlinear and show decreasing returns to scale; after all, corporate philanthropy cannot be expected to increase financial performance in perpetuity. The relationship has also been found to be weaker among companies and industries that are less advertising- or innovation-focused.

Summary

Margolis, Elfenbein, and Walsh concluded that "research must reach beyond simply assessing the magnitude of the corporate social and financial performance relationship; [it] must now show how corporate social performance comes to bear upon corporate financial performance." Put another way: It is time to study mechanisms more systematically. Addressing the hypotheses posed in both these scholarly studies and by traditional investors requires measuring and understanding the operational drivers of business value—business value derived from increased employee engagement, customer loyalty, reputational capital, and opportunities for innovation.

How to attract responsible investors?

A company's cost of capital is the price it pays investors to supply capital for its business activities. It is the rate of return that investors require for investing in a company. If a company attracts a larger pool of potential investors, it can raise capital at a lower cost than its peers, earn a wider profit margin, and enjoy a higher stock-price multiple.

Effect on cost of capital and share prices

Socially responsible investing (SRI)—the practice of investors who think ethically and socially about which stocks to buy, sell, or avoid altogether—has a long history. In its earlier forms, SRI was regarded as a niche investment style. In the first wave of SRI strategies, investors applied negative screening and excluded entire sectors or groups of stocks based on a set of ethical criteria. The next wave of strategies, using positive screening, was introduced by benchmark providers such as the Dow Jones Sustainability Index (DJSI). This selected only the companies that rated highest on a broader set of environmental, social, and governance (ESG) responsibility criteria. The total amount of money invested in traditional SRI is still considered to be relatively small and volatile. In the 2008 Report on Socially Responsible Investing Trends in the United States, The Social Investment Forum estimated that approximately one in every ten dollars of assets under institutional management in the U.S.—an estimated $2.3 trillion out of $24 trillion—was invested in companies that rate high on some measure of social responsibility. Analysts generally estimate that SRI presently makes up no more than 5-10% of all stock market investments. A far more important factor will depend on how much mainstream investors start to recognize and reward performance in corporate social responsibility (CSR). Increasingly, investors are recognizing that responsible corporate performance, when combined with traditional financial analysis, informs their assessments about whether companies are good *financial* investments. This also removes the issue of personal values-based preferences, which can be a slippery slope to navigate, particularly for professional money managers. European institutional investors appear to be leading and adopting this movement more widely. For example, Swedish and Norwegian pension funds, representing close to $1 trillion of combined assets,

> Increasingly, investors are recognizing that responsible corporate performance, when combined with traditional financial analysis, informs their assessments about whether companies are good *financial* investments.

recently signed on to the Sustainable Value Creation Initiative (SVC) to influence companies to improve the social and environmental aspects of their operations, which they believe reduce risks and costs while harnessing and developing business opportunities.[32]

Researchers from the University of British Columbia and the University of Vienna[33] created a model of stock market prices to examine how social investors materially affect those prices. This model determined whether a growing class of socially concerned investors would create incentives for companies to act in a more socially responsible manner by lowering their cost of capital. In their book *Investing for Change*, Augustin Landier and Vinay Nair have applied this model to estimate a back-of-the-envelope relationship between stock-price valuation and the proportion of socially responsible investors in the market. For example, if the amount of SRI capital switches from 10% of the total available capital to 15% in three years, the cost of capital of responsible companies may be lowered by more than 0.8%. Such a drop from, say, a 10.0% return required by investors to 9.2% could increase the valuation of these companies by as much as 11%.[34]

Other researchers have approached this question by examining how substantially stock prices have moved based on SRI-motivated capital flows. SRI funds often track membership in certain specialized benchmarks to identify which companies to invest in. These benchmarks are maintained by index providers such as Dow Jones or FTSE, often in collaboration with ESG research firms. As companies are included or dropped from such indexes, one would expect SRI-linked capital to flow into or out of those stocks. These are potentially abrupt events: if SRI flows are material enough, they could drive stock prices of companies entering indexes to rise, at least temporarily, and those exiting to experience a drop. Researchers have collected large datasets of these events and examined the average stock-price changes, accounting for broader market movements and other factors typically controlled for in event-study methodologies. In recent working papers from the Federal Reserve

Bank of Atlanta and Bank of Finland,[35] researchers looked at the price performance of all stocks between 1990 and 2004 on the announcement that they were dropped from the Domini 400 Social Index. They found that the exiting company experienced a significant abnormal stock-price drop of about 3%. Another research team[36] at the University of Calgary studied additions and deletions of North American stocks to the Dow Jones Sustainability Index from 2002 to 2007. They found that inclusion in this index was valuable for a company, measuring a boost in market value of about 2% compared to stocks that were dropped.

Mainstream responsible investing

Contrary to earlier and more traditional approaches of SRI, which was driven largely by investors' personal values, the case for mainstream institutional investors lies in recognizing that responsible corporate behavior is a proxy for the quality of company management and the extent to which that management is forward-looking and adaptable. Responsible investing (RI) is characterized by the incorporation of social and environmental factors within traditional investment decision-making processes, based on the rationale that such a combined investment framework is more effective for assessing the financial value of companies, particularly over the long term.

The growth and influence of responsible investing will be determined more by the interest of mainstream investors than by traditional SRI funds. In April 2006, former UN Secretary General Kofi Annan launched a global initiative centered on a set of voluntary values and guidelines for asset owners and professionals. The PRI Report on Progress 2008 reported that, as of May 2008, approximately 300 financial institutions representing a total of $15 trillion in professionally managed assets have subscribed to these UN Principles for Responsible Investment. The six principles, listed below, are not prescriptive, but they provide a framework according to which investors can organize and integrate ESG criteria into mainstream investment analysis and ownership practices. Although subscription to these principles does not necessarily mean that all funds already fully comply with them, funds are nevertheless expected to pursue compliance and to report to the UN Secretariat on their progress.

The Six UN Principles for Responsible Investment are:

1. We will incorporate ESG issues into investment analysis and decision-making processes.

2. We will be active owners and incorporate ESG issues into our ownership policies and practices.

3. We will seek appropriate disclosure on ESG issues from the entities in which we invest.

4. We will promote acceptance and implementation of the Principles within the investment industry.

5. We will work together to enhance our effectiveness in implementing the Principles.

6. We will each report on our activities and progress towards implementing the Principles.

The potential impact of responsible investing on how stocks are revalued and corporations behave is huge. If just a third of subscribers implement these principles in their investment process, the combined size of investments linked to some corporate-responsibility criteria would triple. However, the range of screening criteria and rating assessments is wide, in contrast to simple, early SRI approaches like tobacco-industry screens. Professional managers and analysts cite a general view broadly consistent with recognizing "ESG performance as a proxy for management quality, in so far as it reflects the company's ability to respond to long term trends and maintaining a competitive advantage."[37] Much of their specific analysis ultimately relies on the subjective judgment of individual analysts and on proprietary frameworks rather than standardized metrics. A review of the ratings processes of major ESG research firms confirms that while their general principles share much overlap, they do apply subjective metrics and proprietary rating schemes. These ratings generally consider not only the level of philanthropic contributions, but also attempt to account for other factors, such as the innovative quality of giving and the measurement processes involved.

In 1999, Dow Jones & Company launched the first global indexes tracking the stock-price performance of leading sustainability-driven companies worldwide. According to the Dow Jones Sustainable Indexes 2007 Annual Review, asset managers in sixteen countries collectively managed about $6 billion based on the DJSI. Inclusion within the index is based on criteria that are weighted approximately equally for economic, environmental, and social performance, though actual weights differ among industry groups. In order to apply for inclusion in the DJSI, companies must complete a questionnaire—an extensive survey that incorporates both generic as well as industry-specific questions. This information is supplemented by company and third-party documents, personal contact between analysts and company representatives, and additional information from media and NGOs. Companies are ranked within their industry groups and selected for the indexes if they are among the top 10% of sustainability leaders in their respective industry sectors. Although a significant commitment of costs and efforts may be required for collecting the information and completing the survey, companies see the DJSI label as an important mechanism for establishing a reputation in sustainability. The general section of the survey questionnaire is comprised of 51 sets of questions covering economic, environmental, and social issues. Accounting for 3.5% weight in the company's overall score, corporate philanthropy is assessed based, in part, on responses to these questions[38]:

1. Does the company have a system in place to measure the business, social, and reputation/stakeholder impact of its contributions, in order to improve and re-align its philanthropic/social investment strategy?

2. What is the estimated monetary value of its philanthropic contributions/voluntary social investments in cash, employee volunteering, and product donations?

Two other prominent social ratings firms are:

1. KLD Research & Analytics, Inc. (KLD) has conducted research into the ESG performance of listed companies since 1988. Based on KLD's rating indicators, the Domini 400 Social Index was the first socially responsible stock benchmark in America. In 2008, FTSE agreed to co-brand KLD's suite of ESG benchmarks. KLD's research database, SOCRATES, contains ESG reports and ratings on every Russell 3000® and S&P 500® company and is a widely used measure of corporate social responsibility for industry and academic research.

2. Innovest Strategic Value Advisors is another global provider of extra-financial and sustainability-based investment research, institutionally

recognized since 1995. Its Intangible Value Assessment (IVA) model combines performance ratings on 120 sustainability practices, categorized into four major areas: stakeholder capital (relationship with local community, as well as partnerships, supply chain, and human rights); human capital (employee development, labor relations, and health and safety); strategic governance (overall strategy, adaptability, product development and safety); and environment (overall environmental impact, including strategy, governance, management systems, opportunity, and risk).

In 2009, the RiskMetrics Group, a leading provider of financial risk-management products and services to global institutions, announced its intention to acquire Innovest and KLD and to integrate their sustainability research capabilities into its suite of financial risk-management offerings. Responding to its clients' indicated belief[39] that ESG performance is a critical benchmark of companies' risks and long-term value, RiskMetrics has committed to make ESG analysis an integral part of mainstream investment research.

An important effort to standardize corporate non-financial reporting was initiated in 1997 by The Coalition for Environmentally Responsible Economies (CERES), The Tellus Institute, and The United National Environment Program. The Global Reporting Initiative (GRI), which these entities launched through consultation with multiple stakeholder groups, publishes periodically revised reporting guidelines. However, the GRI neither assesses whether company reports conform to those guidelines nor verifies their accuracy, thus potentially reducing the reports' value to investors. Moreover, the growing length of reports may complicate financial analysts' ability to use them effectively.[40] The current set of guidelines, entitled G3, includes performance indicators that fall into one of the following categories: economic (9 indicators), environmental (30), labor practice (14), human rights (9), society performance (8), and product responsibility performance (9). Companies are required to update this data annually.[41] The G3 indicator for community impact, SO1, obliges companies to report the "nature, scope, and effectiveness of any programs and practices that assess and manage the impact of operations on communities, including entering, operating, and exiting." In a review of 72 company reports, the GRI found that "the majority of G3 reporters claim to be reporting in accordance with the G3 Guidelines SO1 indicator; however, in reality only 11% of the G3 reporters fully report according to the SO1 indicator protocol."[42] The reports examined were found to focus mostly on reporting their own performance (as opposed to what changes or benefits occur as a result of their activities) and to emphasize positive community impact without mentioning any negative ones.

Summary

If the criteria applied by social rating firms seem inconsistent and subjective, this may be as much a result of the unevenness and ambiguity of what many companies disclose. It is also unclear to what extent criteria and disclosures are linked to financial value. There is a significant opportunity for companies to lead the industry in developing standards or differentiating themselves to the investor community through their disclosures about philanthropic efforts.

> A high-quality measurement process is a critical input for good management and demonstrates that a company recognizes how its philanthropic strategies can be successful in creating long-term business value.

Documentation of the measurement process should be an important part of establishing quality disclosures and standards. A high-quality measurement process is a critical input for good management and demonstrates that a company recognizes how its philanthropic strategies can be successful in creating long-term business value. The Dow Jones Sustainability Indexes questionnaire also asks if the company has in place a measurement system, although it does not provide guidance about what Dow Jones considers to be a good system. The review and findings summarized in this report suggest that companies could be rated on at least the following criteria:

1. The company has documented high-quality logic models or understanding of the process by which its various types of philanthropic initiatives achieve business benefits.

2. The company has defined business-related outcome metrics, measures them, and has in place a rigorous process to improve or re-align its various philanthropic strategies.

3. The company systematically tracks social outcomes and compares these to targets or benchmarks by which it can monitor whether its philanthropic investments are effective overall.

27 A general formula for the Residual Income Model commonly used in equity valuation reduces the relationship of price-to-book multiples to cost of capital, r; profitability as measured by Return on Equity, ROE; and growth, g: $P/B = 1 + [ROE - r]/[r - g]$.

28 Lev (2001).

29 Margolis, Elfenbein, & Walsh (2007), p. 22.

30 The researchers found that tobacco companies enjoyed 14-21% lower ownership by institutional investors and 15% lower coverage by brokerage analysts.

31 For example, Wang, Choi, & Li (2008) and Lev, Petrovits, & Radhakrishnan (2009) found a decreasing rate of return to philanthropic spending in their sample of companies, while Luo & Bhattacharya (2009) found in their sample that companies enjoy a stronger link between measures of financial and social performance if they are heavy investors in advertising and research and development.

32 See Swedish AP funds join sustainability initiative (*IPE*, 2009, September 11).

33 Heinkel, Kraus, & Zechner (2001).

34 The perpetual-growth model is often represented by the following formula, which assumes a constant, long-term growth rate of earnings: $P = [earnings]/[r - g]$. Substituting an assumption of 10% normal cost of capital and 2% long-term earnings growth (g) and modeling a drop in the cost of capital (r) to 9.2% shows an increase of 11.1% in stock-price valuation. See Landier & Nair (2008).

35 Becchetti, Ciciretti, & Hasan (2009).

36 Robinson, Kleffner, & Bertels (2009).

37 The report by the Asset Management Working Group of the United Nations Environment Programme Finance Initiative and Mercer (October 2007) surveyed the frameworks of several major sell-side research firms.

38 SAM Research (2009). *Corporate Sustainability Assessment Questionnaire*.

39 See press release RiskMetrics Group Announces Acquisition of KLD Research & Analytics, Inc. (2009, November 3). Retrieved from http://www.riskmetrics.com/press/RMG_aquires_KLD

40 Vogel (2005).

41 Global Reporting Initiative (2006).

42 See Global Reporting Initiative, University of Hong Kong and CSR Asia (2008).

Conclusion

Philanthropic initiatives provide novel channels through which companies can meet core business goals and create long-term financial value—by increasing employee engagement, customer loyalty, reputational capital, and market opportunities. These improvements are most effective when corporate giving teams work in concert with existing company operations. However, some companies do not target or measure the business benefits of their philanthropy—possibly because these benefits are intangible or not easily associated with short-term financial profits. Measurement frameworks can be introduced by leveraging models and evidence developed by related business disciplines; they can also help identify key intermediate outcomes that, if targeted, can ultimately yield desired business behaviors and benefits. Scholarly studies have found that these links are not always straightforward, however. It is hoped that the analysis in this report will spark additional research, measurement, and understanding of these mechanisms.

For example, it will be instructive to study how companies test and validate the effects of volunteer programs and other philanthropic activities on employee engagement and behavior. It will also be useful to learn from companies' experiences with estimating cash flows, probabilities, discount rates and other model parameters that affect the valuation of growth opportunities arising from philanthropic projects. Many companies already possess related data and valuable examples. There is much room for those companies to conduct and share thoughtful analyses of methodologies and frameworks without disclosing proprietary business information. This work is not merely academic; it provides actionable, research-based evidence in support of measuring value and promoting more effective alignment of philanthropic programs with core business goals.

A wide range of social impact-assessment frameworks is available in the social sector; many of these frameworks have been put forth by sophisticated private foundations reflecting their unique needs and goals. Given the diversity of missions that nonprofit organizations and funders pursue, there appears to be no single quantitative or qualitative methodology against which performance of all grant types can be evaluated. Which approach a corporate giver should apply will depend on the motivation and focus of its philanthropic program. For example, the appropriate measurement strategy will depend on whether a company seeks to meet communal obligations, build a signature partnership, make a few high-value grants to one cause, make many one-off grants addressing multiple causes—or a combination of these.

> **Measurement is not an unnecessary burden or unrecoverable cost if it adds value.**

Nonprofit organizations face mounting pressure to demonstrate the effectiveness of their programs. Because they can call on internal relevant skills and experiences, companies are in an apt position to help grantees emphasize and take advantage of measurement, both to communicate and improve performance. Measurement is not an unnecessary burden or unrecoverable cost if it adds value. Its value is maximized by organizations that harness it to build and learn from data over time. In a challenging economic period, when organizations seek to reduce overhead expenses of any kind, it is particularly important to distinguish "good" from "bad" overhead and to maintain funding dedicated to the ongoing improvement of philanthropic "bang for the buck."

The investor community increasingly esteems companies with strong community records. Investors reason that such behavior represents the quality and foresight of management. Investors and analysts appreciate disclosures about philanthropic commitments that are comparable, material, and financially relevant. Absent effective industry standards, companies have an opportunity to distinguish themselves in their conversations with the investor community by proposing standards of their own. Part of such a proposal may include detailed insights into the related measurement process, which can help demonstrate understanding of what drives long-term business success, quality of management, and superior potential to create financial value.

The value of corporate philanthropy is measurable; as with many elements of business, however, it cannot always be measured as precisely as we would like.[43] "What gets measured, gets managed" goes the old adage; indeed, measurement plays a crucial role in enabling companies to reach their full potential—both philanthropically and as more successful and sustainable enterprises overall.

---

43 McElhaney (Fall 2008).

Appendices

A. Glossary

Attribution – The assertion that certain events or conditions were, to some extent, caused or influenced by certain other events or conditions. This means a reasonable connection can be made between a specific outcome and the actions and outputs of a policy, program, intervention, or initiative.

Balanced Scorecard – A process developed in the early 1990s by Robert Kaplan and David Norton for translating an organization's mission and strategy statements into a comprehensive system for measuring organizational performance. Balanced scorecards collect diverse information intended to "balance" the traditional, but narrow, financial view of performance. They are a tool for helping managers understand how their organizations are performing and translate strategy into action. According to this approach, performance measures should be defined in four areas: (1) finance, (2) customer satisfaction, (3) internal processes, and (4) innovation and learning for employees. The selected measures are specific to the organization and chosen to reflect the drivers believed to be most important to understanding success.

Baseline – A state of the world without the program and that can be compared to the world with the program in place. A starting point for assessing changes in performance and for establishing objectives or targets for future performance.

Before-After Designs (or Pre-Post Designs) – An evaluation that involves the measurement of "outcome" indicators (e.g., arrest rates or attitudes) prior to implementation of the treatment and re-measurement after implementation. Any change in the measure is ascribed to the treatment. This design provides a significant improvement over the one-shot study because it measures change in the factor(s) to be impacted. However, the design does not correct for the possibility that some factor or factors external to the treatment actually caused the change.

Benchmark – A level of achievement against which organizations can measure their progress. Benchmarks may be used for comparisons of organizational processes against an internal or external standard.

Causation – The conditional statement of inference that the change in a single variable is responsible for a resulting change in another variable.

Common Measures – Standard measures of impact (outcomes) that can be used across a variety of programs in a field of study (e.g., children's I.Q. scores, within the field of education).

Comparison Group – A group of individuals whose characteristics are similar to those of a program's participants. These individuals may not receive any services, or they may receive a different set of services, activities, or products; in no instance do they receive the same services as those being evaluated. As part of the evaluation process, the experimental group (i.e., those receiving program services) and the comparison group are assessed to determine which types of services, activities, or products provided by the program produced the expected changes.

---

*Adapted from: (1) Office of Policy, Economics and Innovation, Evaluation Support Division, U.S., *EPA Program Evaluation Glossary*, http://www.epa.gov/evaluate/glossary/all-esd.htm; (2) Melinda T. Tuan, Bill & Melinda Gates Foundation (2008, December 15), *Measuring and/or Estimating Social Value Creation: Insights Into Eight Integrated Cost Approaches*; (3) CFA Institute Centre for Financial Market Integrity (2008), *Environmental, Social, and Governance Factors at Listed Companies: A Manual for Investors*; (4) W. K. Kellogg Foundation (January 2004), *Logic Model Development Guide*; and (5) United States Government Accountability Office (May 2005), *Performance Measurement and Evaluation: Definitions and Relationships*, GAO-05-739SP.

Conjoint Analysis – A survey and analytical approach to quantify consumers' values associated with different product attributes using multivariate statistical techniques. Participants compare products to establish their relative preferences, which are then used to quantify the importance of different attributes.

Control Group – A group whose characteristics are similar to those of the program's treated participants but who do not receive the program services, products, or activities being evaluated. Participants are randomly assigned to either the experimental group (those receiving program services/treatment) or the control group. A control group is used to assess the effect of program activities on participants who are receiving the services, products, or activities being evaluated. The same information is collected for people in the control group and those in the experimental group.

Control Variable – A variable that is held constant or whose impact is removed in the statistical model in order to analyze the relationship between other variables without interference.

Corporate Social Responsibility (CSR) – Considers the impact of a company on society as a whole, based on how the company takes responsibility for the effect of its activities on a number of stakeholders: employees, the communities in which the company operates, the environment, etc.; in other words, not just on its shareowners.

Cost-Benefit Analysis (CBA) – Takes the perspective of society as a whole and considers the costs and dollar-valued outcomes aggregated across all stakeholders (including government sector, individuals as taxpayers, program participants, private individuals, and the rest of society). The output from cost-benefit analysis can be measures of net benefits (i.e., benefits minus costs), the ratio of benefits to cost (benefit-cost ratios), or the internal rate of return (the rate of growth a project is expected to generate). By requiring comprehensive measurement of costs and program impact and the ability to place a dollar value on program impact across stakeholders, CBA is the most demanding of the cost-and-outcome analysis approaches. At the same time, it is also the most comprehensive in providing a full accounting of the net benefits to both stakeholders and society as a whole.

Cost-Effectiveness Analysis (CEA) – The calculation of a ratio of cost-to-non-monetary benefit. The focus may be on one domain of impact (e.g., crime or student achievement) or multiple areas of impact. However, measures of cost-effectiveness can account for only one area of program impact at a time. Since the impact of programs is measured in the program's respective natural units (e.g., life years improved or children graduating from high school), unless those units are common across all areas of impact, it is not possible to aggregate across them.

Counterfactual – The hypothetical situation that would occur in the absence of the social program or if the target group were not exposed to the program.

Customer Lifetime Value – The net present value of the profit an organization expects to realize from a customer for the duration of their relationship. Customer lifetime value focuses on customers as assets rather than sources of revenue. The volume of purchases made, customer-retention rates, and profit margins are factors taken into account in calculating customer lifetime value.

Customer Loyalty – Feelings or attitudes that incline a customer to return to a company, shop, or outlet or to re-purchase a particular product, service, or brand.

Dashboard Reporting – A dashboard is a visualization tool that provides graphical depictions of current key performance indicators in order to enable faster response to changes in areas such as sales, customer relations, performance assessments, and inventory levels.

Dependent Variable – A variable that is believed to be predictable or caused by one or more other variables called independent variables.

Disability-Adjusted Life Year (DALY) – The DALY relies on an acceptance that the most appropriate measure of the effects of chronic illness is time—both time lost due to premature death and time spent disabled by disease. One DALY, therefore, is equal to one year of healthy life lost. When calculated, the DALY is the number of years of life lost due to premature death (compared to a standard life expectancy) plus the years of life lived in a state of less than full health. The principal difference between Quality-Adjusted Life Years (QALYs) and DALYs is that QALY weightings are derived by asking patients to rate their health status, whereas in DALYs the weightings are derived by asking health experts or the general public to rate a whole series of health-related states (e.g., if one lost a limb, became blind, or were confined to a wheelchair).

Discount Rate – The discount rate is a financial metric that may be used to determine the present value of future payments or expenditures.

Discounting – The practice of weighing or valuing outcomes that occur sooner more than outcomes that are delayed. It is obvious why this should be so with money. One would rather have $1,000 today than $1,000 next year, because if a person had $1,000 today he or she could invest it and have more than $1,000 next year. The same logic of discounting or applying time preferences can be applied to non-monetary outcomes.

Efficient Capital Market – A stock market in which all relevant new information is very quickly reflected in a stock's price. Investors should not expect to earn an abnormal return.

Employee Engagement – A heightened emotional connection that an employee feels for his or her organization and that influences the employee to exert greater discretionary effort in performing his or her work.

Environmental, Social, and Governance (ESG) – ESG-related issues that investors are considering in the context of corporate behavior. ESG issues are typically considered non-financial or non-quantifiable in nature and have a medium-to-long-term time frame in their effect on a company.

Expected Value – A term used by mathematicians to represent the average amount one "expects" to be the outcome of a random trial when identical odds are repeated many times.

Explanatory Factors – Influences that might affect an organization's or person's performance. Usually the term is used to refer to factors outside the control of the organization or person and that have an effect on performance data.

Field Experiments – Research conducted in the actual setting environment (i.e., outside the laboratory).

Focus Group – A marketing research technique for qualitative data that involves a small group of people (e.g., 6-10) who share a common set of characteristics (e.g., demographics, attitudes, etc.) and participate in a discussion of predetermined topics led by a moderator.

Granger Causality Test – A statistical technique developed by econometrician Clive Granger (who won a Nobel Prize in Economics) for determining whether one time series is useful in forecasting another.

Halo Effect – This refers to the tendency to rate a person's skills and talents or a company's capabilities in many areas based upon evaluation of a single factor. It creates bias by increasing an observer's tendency to rate, perhaps unintentionally, certain objects, persons, or companies in a manner that reflects what was anticipated.

Impact – The long-term sustainable and attributable change due to a specific intervention or set of interventions. It is the ultimate effect of the program on the problem or condition that the program or activity was supposed to do something about.

Impact Evaluation – Assesses the net effect of a program by comparing program outcomes with an estimate of what would have happened in the absence of a program. Employed when other external factors are known to influence the program's outcomes, in order to isolate the program's contribution to achievements or its objectives.

Inputs – The resources used to run the program: money, people, facilities, and equipment.

Logic Model – A systematic and visual way to present and share your understanding of the relationships among the resources you have to operate your program, the activities you plan, and the changes or results you hope to achieve. *Logic model* is frequently used interchangeably with *program theory* in the evaluation field. Logic models can alternatively be referred to as theory because they describe the relationships between the strategy and tactics adopted by the program and the social benefits the program is expected to produce:

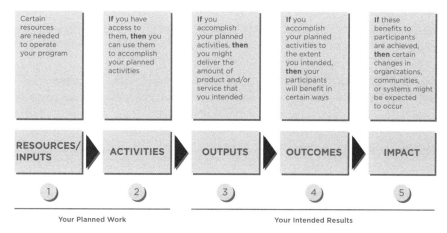

Basic Logic Model. Source: W. K. Kellogg Foundation Logic Model Development Guide.

The most basic logic model is a picture of how you believe your program will work. It uses words and/or pictures to describe the sequence of activities thought to effect change and how these activities are linked to the results the program is expected to achieve.

PLANNED WORK describes what resources you think you need to implement your program and what you intend to do.

• Resources (or Inputs) include the human, financial, organizational, and community resources a program has available to direct toward doing the work.

• Program Activities (or Interventions) are what the program does with the resources. Activities are the processes, tools, events, technology, and actions that are an intentional part of the program implementation to bring about the intended program changes or results.

INTENDED RESULTS include all of the program's desired results.

- Outputs are the direct products of program activities and may include types, levels, and targets of services to be delivered by the program.
- Outcomes are the specific changes in program participants' behavior, knowledge, skills, status, and level of functioning.
- Impact is the fundamental intended or unintended change occurring in organizations, communities, or systems as a result of program activities over the long term. Impact often occurs after the conclusion of project funding.

Longitudinal Study – A research study conducted over time by observing a certain sample set to understand developmental trends. May use the same sample set over decades or may utilize a new sample at set intervals.

Meta-Analysis – The systematic analysis of a set of existing evaluations of similar programs in order to draw general conclusions, develop support for hypotheses, and/or produce an estimate of overall program effects.

Motivation-Crowding Theory – A psychological finding that suggests that external incentives such as monetary rewards or punishments may undermine intrinsic motivation. An employee who is intrinsically motivated is driven by internal emotional factors such as prestige, self-respect, feeling of accomplishment, and/or a sense of belonging with his or her work group or organization.

Natural Unit – Outcomes measured in non-monetary terms and naturally associated with the program's objectives. Natural units are typically used in cost-effectiveness analysis as the denominator of the cost-effectiveness ratio (e.g., cost per natural unit x). Examples of natural units include life years saved and children graduating from high school.

Negative Screening – An investment approach that excludes some companies or sectors from the possible investment universe based on criteria relating to their policies, actions, products, or services. Investments that do not meet the minimum standards of the screen are not included in the investment portfolio.

Net Present Value (NPV) – The traditional method for quantifying the financial attractiveness of a project. NPV, also called *discounted cash flow* (DCF), represents the amount in today's dollars (present value) by which all income expected from the project exceeds all costs. NPV computes the present value for a project by discounting estimated future incremental cash inflows and outflows. Typically, the discount rate is chosen to represent a required rate of return or target yield for the capital invested. To calculate a project's NPV accurately, it is necessary to estimate the life-cycle cash flows that would result from executing the project, including not only the project costs but also all of its financial benefits, such as future cost savings, future operating costs, and any "exit" costs or values.

One-Shot Case Study – A study involving the measurement of an identified "outcome" after a treatment or program has been implemented. However, there are no pre-program or other comparison measures taken or available. Without a comparison measure, there are no means for inferring that the "outcome" was actually influenced by the treatment or program.

Organizational Identification – Measures the degree to which individuals define themselves as members of an organization, believe they and the organization are one entity, and possess or share the organization's values.

Outcomes – The changes that occur over time following activities (interventions) or outputs. Outcomes can be measured at a variety of levels: individual, organizational, community, system, funding stream, etc. Outcomes may be direct or indirect. Direct outcomes follow from outputs (e.g., getting a job) while indirect outcomes follow from direct outcomes (e.g., increase in income due to a job gained).

Outputs – The direct and tangible products of an activity (e.g., the number of people trained).

Performance Measurement – The ongoing monitoring and reporting of program accomplishments, particularly progress toward pre-established goals. Performance measures may address the type or level of program activities conducted (process), the direct products and services delivered by a program (outputs), or the results of those products and services (outcomes).

Positive Screening – An investment approach that includes some companies or sectors from the possible investment universe based on criteria relating to their policies, actions, products, or services. Investments that meet the minimum standards of the screen are included in the investment portfolio.

Program Evaluations – These are individual systematic studies conducted periodically or on an ad hoc basis to assess how well a program is working. They are often conducted by experts external to the program as well as by program managers. A program evaluation typically examines achievement of program objectives in the context of other aspects of program performance or in the context in which it occurs.

Quality-Adjusted Life Year (QALY) – A single measure of health outcome that simultaneously captures gains from reduced morbidity (**quality**-of-life gains) and reduced mortality (**quantity**-of-life gains). QALYs are calculated by multiplying the number of years of life that would be added by the intervention by the improvement in quality of life from that intervention (measured on a scale between 0 and 1 where 1 is a state of full health and 0 is the worst possible health state). The principal difference between QALYs and Disability-Adjusted Life Years (DALYs) is that QALY weightings are derived by asking patients to rate their health status, whereas in DALYs the weightings are derived by asking health experts or the general public to rate a whole series of health-related states (e.g., if one lost a limb, became blind, or were confined to a wheelchair).

Quasi-Experimental Designs – Evaluation research that includes a comparison group chosen on the basis of matched characteristics but not random assignment. Considered to deliver somewhat less certainty than results from randomized experimental design evaluations, but more certainty than pre-post (or before-after) evaluations. Used when finding randomly assigned groups is not possible or appropriate.

Randomized Experimental Designs – Evaluation research conducted whereby the control and treatment groups are as similar as possible except for participation in the program. In experimental evaluations, individuals are randomly assigned to the control group (i.e., the group that receives no new program services or faces the status quo) or the treatment group (i.e., the group that receives the program services or faces the policy alternative). Thus, any differences can be attributed to the impact of the program or policy.

Real-Options Analysis – A method for valuing projects and assets based on concepts originally developed to value financial options. Real-options analysis is most useful for large capital budget decisions in situations involving significant uncertainties (especially market uncertainties) and where management has flexibility to adapt decisions to unexpected developments. For example, real-options analysis is often used for mergers and acquisitions, facility-expansion decisions, oil exploration, contract valuation, and prioritizing research and development projects. The options inherent in physical assets are termed "real" to distinguish them from classic financial options. Traditional financial valuation methods, including net present value (NPV), typically undervalue projects because they fail to account adequately for the value of management flexibility to exercise projects' inherent options.

Representative Sample – A sample that has approximately the same distribution of characteristics as the population from which it was drawn.

Response Bias – Erroneous answers given to an interviewer's questions due to misinterpretation by the participant or to the participant responding in such a way that he or she believes the interviewer would like him or her to answer (as opposed to how he or she would answer if being honest). Can occur both deliberately and unintentionally.

Return on Investment (ROI) – The ratio of project income to project cost, reflecting money gained or lost on an investment relative to the amount of money invested. Typically, project income is the average annual net income from the project and project cost is the total invested capital. ROI is widely used in the private sector, both to justify a planned project and to evaluate the extent to which the desired return was achieved.

Scenario Analysis – A process used in decision-making. Analyzes future outcomes by considering a series of alternative possibilities (scenarios) and their implications.

Signature Program – A philanthropic project that represents a major investment of firm resources, often in a long-term partnership with nonprofit organizations. Is meant to generate impact consistent with the company's self-definition, values, and goals for business growth. Related decisions are typically approved at the executive or board level and the program involves senior management engagement; contributions of company product, services, expertise, and relationships; and access to corporate resources such as training or technologies. Generally a large commitment sustained over many years.

Six Sigma – First utilized in Japan and pioneered in America in the 1970s by Motorola and GE, Six Sigma is a business methodology for improving the quality of business process outputs. The methodology aims to identify and remove the causes of defects (errors or variations in process outputs) that lead to customer dissatisfaction. There are five steps (represented by the acronym DMAIC) in the methodology: (1) define the customer and business goals for the process, (2) measure defects in the performance of the current process, (3) analyze the data to identify root causes of defects, (4) improve the process to reduce defects, and (5) control the variables that cause defects. *Six Sigma* refers to a concept in statistics for measuring how far a given process deviates from perfection and suggests that errors be reduced to a few per million, at most.

Social Return on Investment (SROI) – A term popularized by REDF in the late 1990s and that now has widespread use in both the nonprofit and increasingly for-profit sectors for describing approaches to estimating or calculating the social output or outcomes or impact of a program or enterprise. There is currently no standard definition for SROI, although it is widely referenced in the work of nonprofits, philanthropy, and socially responsible businesses. SROI measures an organization's added value by calculating the social, environmental, and economic benefits it creates and by attributing to these a financial value.

Socially Responsible Investing (SRI) – An investment process that seeks to achieve social and environmental objectives alongside financial objectives.

Triple Bottom Line – The notion of measuring a company's success by more than just financial metrics or the traditional "bottom line." The triple bottom line attempts to incorporate a measurement of a company's social and environmental performance (and its effectiveness in addressing the needs of stakeholders beyond shareowners) into an overall measure of corporate success.

United Nations Environment Programme Finance Initiative (UNEP FI) – A global partnership between the United Nations Environment Programme and the private financial sector. UNEP FI works closely with the 170 financial institutions that are signatories to the UNEP FI Statements as well as with a range of partner organizations to develop and promote links among the environment, sustainability, and financial performance. Through regional activities, a comprehensive work program, training programs, and research, UNEP FI carries out its mission to identify, promote, and realize the adoption of best environmental and sustainability practice at all levels of financial institution operations.

United Nations Principles for Responsible Investment (PRI) – A series of investing principles drafted by institutional investors who believe that ESG factors can affect the performance of investment portfolios. The principles support the signatories' belief that investors fulfilling their fiduciary (or equivalent) duty must give appropriate consideration to these factors; the principles also provide a framework for making access to ESG information more widely available and for incorporating the information into the decision-making process.

Validation – A survey-integrity safeguard whereby respondents are contacted to confirm their survey responses.

B. References

Acumen Fund (January 2007). *The best available charitable option: Acumen Fund's approach*. Retrieved from http://www.acumenfund.org/uploads/assets/documents/BACO%20Concept%20Paper%20final_B1cNOVEM.pdf

The Alliance for Effective Social Investing (2009). *Nonprofit social value assessment questions*. Retrieved from http://www.alleffective.org/docs/Nonprofit-Social-Value-Assessment-Questions-Version7.pdf

Ashforth, B. E., & Mael, F. (1989). Social identity theory and the organization. *Academy of Management Review, 14*(1), 20-39.

The Asset Management Working Group of the United Nations Environment Programme Finance Initiative and Mercer (October 2007). *Demystifying responsible investment performance: A review of key academic and broker research on ESG factors*. Retrieved from http://www.unepfi.org/fileadmin/documents/Demystifying_Responsible_Investment_Performance_01.pdf

Bartel, C. A. (2001). Social comparisons in boundary-spanning work: Effects of community outreach on members' organizational identity and identification. *Administrative Science Quarterly, 46*, 379-413.

Basil, D. Z., & Weber, D. (2006). Values motivation and concern for appearances: The effect of personality traits on responses to corporate social responsibility. *International Journal of Nonprofit and Voluntary Sector Marketing, 11*, 61-72.

Becchetti, L., Ciciretti R., & Hasan, I. (2009). *Corporate social responsibility and shareholder's value: An event study analysis (FRB of Atlanta working paper no. 2007-6)*. Retrieved from http://papers.ssrn.com/sol3/papers.cfm?abstract_id=928557

Becker-Olsen, K. L., & Hill, R. (2005). The impact of perceived corporate social responsibility on consumer behavior. *Center for Responsible Business Working Paper Series 27*. Berkeley, CA: University of California, Berkeley.

Bergami, M., & Bagozzi, R. P. (2000). Self-categorization, affective commitment and group self-esteem as distinct aspects of social identity. *British Journal of Social Psychology, 39*, 555-577.

Bhattacharya, C. B., & Sen, S. (Fall 2004). Doing better at doing good: When, why and how consumers respond to corporate social initiatives. *California Management Review, 47*(1), 9-24. Retrieved from http://smgpublish.bu.edu/cb/CMR2004.pdf

Bhattacharya, C. B., Sen S., & Korschun, D. (Winter 2008). Using corporate social responsibility to win the war for talent. *MIT Sloan Management Review, 49*(2), 37-44. Retrieved from http://sloanreview.mit.edu/the-magazine/files/saleable-pdfs/49215.pdf

Bone, P. F., & Ellen, P. S. (1992). The generation and consequences of communication-evoked imagery. *Journal of Consumer Research, 19*(1), 93-104.

Boston College Center for Corporate Citizenship and McKinsey & Company (2009). *How virtue creates value for business and society: Investigating the value of environmental, social and governance activities*. Retrieved from http://www.bcccc.net/index.cfm?fuseaction=document.showDocumentByID&DocumentID=1269

Bradach, J. L., Tierney, T. J., & Stone, N. (December 2008). Delivering on the promise of nonprofits. *Harvard Business Review*, *86*(12), 88-97. Retrieved from http://www.isae.org/sections/documents/DeliveringonthePromiseofNonprofits.pdf

Bruch, H., & Walter, F. (Fall 2005). The keys to rethinking corporate philanthropy. *MIT Sloan Management Review*, *47*(1), 49-55. Retrieved from http://sloanreview.mit.edu/the-magazine/files/saleable-pdfs/47111.pdf

The Center on Philanthropy at Indiana University (May 2007). *Corporate philanthropy: The age of integration*. Indianapolis, IN: Indiana University. Retrieved from http://www.philanthropy.iupui.edu/Research/Corporate%20giving-Target%20project%20July%202007.pdf

Charlton, K., & Osterweil, C. (Fall 2005). Measuring return on investment in executive education: A quest to meet client needs or pursuit of the holy grail? *The Ashridge Journal*, 6-13. Retrieved from http://www.ashridge.org.uk/Website/Content.nsf/FileLibrary/FC30125A4420D12B8025760 20039C093/$file/MeasuringROI.pdf

Christiaens, M. (2008). *Managing reputational risk (Deloitte risk management brief)*. Belgium: Deloitte Enterprise Risk Services. Retrieved from http://www.deloitte.com/assets/Dcom-Belgium/Local%20Assets/Documents/ERS_ManagingReputationalRisk_Sept2008.pdf

Chronicle of Philanthropy (2009, July 13). *Charity Navigator's New Course*. Retrieved from http://philanthropy.com/giveandtake/index.php?id=1123

Chronicle of Philanthropy Conference Notebook (September 2009). Retrieved from http://philanthropy.com/news/monthlyconference/2009/09

Committee Encouraging Corporate Philanthropy and McKinsey & Company (2008). *Business's social contract: Capturing the corporate philanthropy opportunity*. Retrieved from http://www.corporatephilanthropy.org/pdfs/research_reports/SocialContract.pdf

Committee Encouraging Corporate Philanthropy (2009). *Corporate giving standard: 2009 survey guide*. Retrieved from http://www.corporatephilanthropy.org/pdfs/benchmarking_tools/surveyguide.pdf

Cone (2004). *Cone corporate citizenship study*. Retrieved from http://www.coneinc.com/content1086

The Conference Board (2006). *Philanthropy and business—The changing agenda* (Report #1389-06-RR). Abstract retrieved from http://www.conference-board.org/utilities/pressDetail.cfm?press_ID=2877

Damodaran, A. (January 2006). *Dealing with intangibles: Valuing brand names, flexibility and patents*. Retrieved from http://www.stern.nyu.edu/~adamodar/pdfiles/papers/intangibles.pdf

Deloitte LLP (2004). *Deloitte volunteer IMPACT survey*.

Dow Jones Sustainability Indexes (September 2009). *Dow Jones Sustainability World Index Guide, Version 11.1*. Retrieved from http://www.sustainability-index.com/djsi_pdf/publications/Guidebooks/DJSI_Guidebook_World_80.pdf

Du, S., Bhattacharya, C. B., & Sen, S. (2007). Reaping relational rewards from corporate social responsibility: The role of competitive positioning. *International Journal of Research in Marketing*, *24*, 224-241. Retrieved from http://smgpublish.bu.edu/cb/IJRM731.pdf

Eccles, R. G., Newquist, S. C., & Schatz, R. (February 2007). Reputation and its risks. *Harvard Business Review*, *85*(22), 104-114. Retrieved from http://annenberg.usc.edu/images/pdfs/current/hbr.jan2007-reputation-article.pdf

Edmans, A. (2008, December 30). *Does the stock market fully value intangibles? Employee satisfaction and equity prices*. Retrieved from http://papers.ssrn.com/sol3/papers.cfm?abstract_id=985735

Ellen, P. S., Webb, D. J., & Mohr, L. A. (2006). Building corporate associations: Consumer attributions for corporate socially responsible programs. *Journal of the Academy of Marketing Science*, *34*(2), 147-158.

Epstein, M. J. (2008). *Making sustainability work: Best practices in managing and measuring corporate social, environmental, and economic impact*. UK: Greenleaf Publishing Ltd.

Faleye, O., & Trahan, E. (May 2006). *Is what's best for employees best for shareholders?* Retrieved from http://papers.ssrn.com/sol3/papers.cfm?abstract_id=888180

Fisman, R., Heal, G., & Nair, V. N. (2007). *A model of corporate philanthropy*. Retrieved from http://knowledge.wharton.upenn.edu/papers/1331.pdf

Fombrun, C. J., Gardberg, N. A., & Barnett, M. L. (2000). Opportunity platforms and safety nets: Corporate citizenship and reputational risk. *Business and Society Review*, *105*(1), 85-106. Retrieved from http://www.www.reputationinstitute.com/press/fombrunetal2002.pdf

Frey, B. S., & Jegen, R. (2001). Motivation-crowding theory: A survey of empirical evidence. *Journal of Economic Surveys*, *15*, 589-611.

Gardberg, N. A., & Fombrun, C. J. (2006). Corporate citizenship: Creating intangible assets across institutional environments. *Academy of Management Review*, *31*(2), 329-346. Retrieved from http://www.reputationinstitute.com/press/06-AMR_Gardberg_Fombrun%20AMR.pdf

Global Reporting Initiative (2006). *Sustainability reporting guidelines, version 3.0*. Retrieved from http://www.globalreporting.org/ReportingFramework/ReportingFrameworkDownloads/

Global Reporting Initiative, the University of Hong Kong, and CSR Asia (2008). *Reporting on community impact*. Retrieved from http://www.globalreporting.org/CurrentPriorities/CommunityImpacts/

Godfrey, P. C., Merrill C. B., & Hansen, J. M. (2009). The relationship between corporate social responsibility and shareholder value: An empirical test of the risk management hypothesis. *Strategic Management Journal*, *30*, 425-445. Abstract retrieved from http://rmrr.com/pdf/Godfrey—Corporate%20Social%20Responsibility%20and%20Shareholder%20Value.pdf

Heal, G. (2008). *When principles pay: corporate social responsibility and the bottom line*. New York, NY: Columbia Business School Press.

Heinkel, R., Kraus, A., & Zechner, J. (2001). The effect of green investment on corporate behavior. *Journal of Financial and Quantitative Analysis*, *36*(4), 431-449

Hills, G., & Mahmud, A. (September 2007). *Volunteering for impact: Best practices in international corporate volunteering*. Boston, MA: FSG. Retrieved from http://www.fsg-impact.org/ideas/item/536

Holmes, S., & Moir, L. (2007). Developing a conceptual framework to identify corporate innovations through engagement with nonprofit stakeholders. *Corporate Governance*, *7*(4), 414-422. Retrieved from http://www.eabis.org/index2.php?option=com_docman&gid=9&task=doc_view

Hong, H., & Kacperczyk, M. (2008). *The price of sin: The effects of social norms on markets.* Retrieved from http://papers.ssrn.com/sol3/papers.cfm?abstract_id=766465

IPE (2009, September 11). *Swedish AP funds join sustainability initiative.* Retrieved from http://ipe.com/articles/print.php?id=32664

Jones, D. A. (2007). *Corporate volunteer programs and employee responses: How serving the community also serves the company.* Socially Responsible Values on Organizational Behavior Interactive Paper Session at the 67th annual meeting of the Academy of Management, Philadelphia, PA.

Kanter, R. M. (1999). From spare change to real change: The social sector as beta site for business innovation. *Harvard Business Review, 77*(3), 122-132.

Kaplan, R. S. (Spring 2001). Strategic performance measurement and management in nonprofit organizations. *Nonprofit Management and Leadership, 11*(3), 353-370. Retrieved from ftp://ftp.unibocconi.it/pub/corsi/ipas/Archivio_A_A_06_07/8126/materiale_didattico/9_kaplan.pdf

Karoly, L. A. (2008). *Valuing benefits in benefit-cost studies of social programs.* Santa Monica, CA: RAND Corporation. Retrieved from http://www.rand.org/pubs/technical_reports/2008/RAND_TR643.sum.pdf

KLD Research and Analytics (2007). *Environmental, social and governance ratings criteria. SOCRATES: The corporate social ratings monitor.* Retrieved from http://www.kld.com/research/ratings_indicators.html

Kramer, M., & Pfitzer, M. (2007). *From insight to action: New direction in evaluation. Research synopsis for social sector funders.* Boston, MA: FSG. Retrieved from http://www.fsg-impact.org/ideas/pdf/488_FromInsighttoAction_NewDirectionsinFoundationEvaluation.pdf

Landier, A., & Nair, V. B. (2009). *Investing for change: Profit from responsible investment.* Oxford, UK: Oxford University Press.

Lev, B. (2001). *Intangibles: Management, measurement and reporting.* Washington, DC: Brookings Institution Press.

Lev, B., Petrovits, C., & Radhakrishnan, S. (2009). Is doing good good for you? How corporate charitable contributions enhance revenue growth. *Strategic Management Review,* forthcoming. Retrieved from http://papers.ssrn.com/sol3/papers.cfm?abstract_id=920502

Li, J., & Rugman, A. M. (2007). Real options and the theory of foreign direct investment. *International Business Review, 16,* 687-712.

Logan, D., & Tuffrey, M. (2000). *Assessing the impact: Using the London Benchmarking Group model to assess how the community and the company benefit from corporate community involvement.* London, UK: Charities Aid Foundation.

Luo, X., & Bhattacharya, C. B. (2006). Corporate social responsibility, customer satisfaction, and market value. *Journal of Marketing, 70,* 1-18. Retrieved from http://smgpublish.bu.edu/cb/JM2006.pdf

Luo, X., & Bhattacharya, C. B. (2009). The debate over doing good: Corporate social performance, strategic marketing levers, and firm-idiosyncratic risk. *Journal of Marketing,* forthcoming. Retrieved from http://smgpublish.bu.edu/cb/jm2009.pdf

Luhtanen, R., & Crocker, J. (1992). A collective self-esteem scale: Self-evaluation of one's social identity. *Personality and Social Psychology Bulletin, 18,* 302-318.

Margolis, J. D., Elfenbein, H. A., & Walsh, J. P. (2007). *Does it pay to be good? A meta-analysis and redirection of research on the relationship between corporate social and financial performance*. Retrieved from http://stakeholder.bu.edu/2007/Docs/Walsh,%20Jim%20Does%20It%20Pay%20to%20Be%20Good.pdf

McAllister, D. J. (1995). Affect- and cognition-based trust as foundations for interpersonal cooperation in organizations. *Academy of Management Journal, 38*, 24-59.

McElhaney, K. (Fall 2008). Measuring what matters? Evaluating CSR's return on investment. *Leading Perspectives, BSR Conferences 2008 Special Issue*, 10-17. Retrieved from http://www.bsr.org/research/leading-perspectives.cfm

McLaughlin, C., Levy, J., Noonan, K., & Rosqueta, K. (February 2009). *Lifting the burden of malaria: An investment guide for impact-driven philanthropy*. Philadelphia, PA: The Center for High Impact Philanthropy, University of Pennsylvania. Retrieved from http://www.impact.upenn.edu/our_work/Malaria-ExecutiveSummary.html

Nelson, J., & Jenkins, B. (2006). *Investing in social innovation: Harnessing the potential of partnership between corporations and social entrepreneurs (Corporate Social Responsibility Initiative working paper no. 20)*. Cambridge, MA: Harvard University John F. Kennedy School of Government. Retrieved from http://www.ksg.harvard.edu/m-rcbg/CSRI/publications/workingpaper_20_nelson_jenkins.pdf

Orlitzky, M. Benjamin, J. D. (2001). Corporate social performance and firm risk: A Meta-analytic review. *Business Society, 40*, 369-396.

Phillips, J. (2005). *Investing in your company's human capital*. New York, NY: AMACOM.

Reichheld, F. F. (2003). The one number you need to grow. *Harvard Business Review, 81*(12), 46-54.

Reichheld, F. F., & Sasser, W. (1990). Zero defects: quality comes to services. *Harvard Business Review, 68*(5), 105-111.

Rhodes, H. J., Noonan, K., & Rosqueta, K. (December 2008). *Pathways to student success:*

A guide to translating good intentions into meaningful impact. Philadelphia, PA: The Center for High Impact Philanthropy, University of Pennsylvania. Retrieved from http://www.impact.upenn.edu/our_work/Pathways-ExecutiveSummary.html

Robinson, M. J., Kleffner, A., & Bertels, S. (2009). *The value of reputation for corporate social responsibility: Empirical evidence*. Retrieved from http://www.northernfinance.org/2008/papers/221.pdf

SAM Research (2009). *Corporate sustainability assessment questionnaire*. Retrieved from https://secure2.sam-group.com/online/documents/testcompany.pdf

Sawhill, J. C., & Williamson, D. (Spring 2001). Mission impossible? Measuring success in nonprofit organizations. *Nonprofit Management and Leadership, 11*(3), 371-386.

Sen, S., & Bhattacharya, C. B. (May 2001). Does doing good always lead to doing better? Consumer reactions to corporate social responsibility. *Journal of Marketing Research, 38*, 225-244. Retrieved from http://smgpublish.bu.edu/cb/jmr2001.pdf

Smith, V., & Langford, P. (2009). Evaluating the impact of corporate social responsibility programs on consumers. *Journal of Management and Organization, 15*, 97-109.

Tropp, L. R., & Wright, S. C. (1999). Ingroup identification as the inclusion of ingroup in the self. *Personality and Social Psychology Bulletin, 5*, 585-600.

Tuan, M. T. (2008). *Measuring and/or estimating social value creation: Insights into eight integrated cost approaches*. Seattle, WA: Bill & Melinda Gates Foundation. Retrieved from http://www.gatesfoundation.org/learning/Pages/december-2008-measuring-estimating-social-value-creation-report-summary.aspx

United Way of America (1996). *Measuring program outcomes: A practical approach*.

The Urban Institute and The Center for What Works (December 2006). *Building a common outcome framework to measure nonprofit performance*. Retrieved from http://www.urban.org/UploadedPDF/411404_Nonprofit_Performance.pdf

Van Dyne, L., Graham, J. W., & Dienesch, R. M. (1994). Organizational citizenship behavior: Construct redefinition, measurement, and validation. *Academy of Management Journal*, *37*, 765-802.

Vogel, D. (2005). *The market for virtue: The potential and limits of corporate social responsibility*. Washington, DC: Brookings Institution Press.

Wang, H., Choi, J., & Li, J. (January-February 2008). Too little or too much? Untangling the relationship between corporate philanthropy and firm financial performance. *Organization Science*, *19*(1), 143-159. Retrieved from http://www.bm.ust.hk/mgmt/staff/papers/too%20little.pdf

Warhurst, A. (2008, December 8). The Future of Corporate Philanthropy. *Business Week*. Retrieved from http://www.businessweek.com/globalbiz/content/dec2008/gb2008128_757524.htm

Weibel, A., Rost, K., & Osterloh, M. (2007). *Crowding-out of intrinsic motivation—Opening the black box*. Retrieved from http://papers.ssrn.com/sol3/papers.cfm?abstract_id=957770

Weinstein, M., with Lamy, C. (2008). *Measuring success: How Robin Hood estimates the impact of grants*. New York, NY: Robin Hood Foundation. Retrieved from http://www.robinhood.org/media/169437/2009_metrics_paper.pdf

W. K. Kellogg Foundation (January 1998). *W. K. Kellogg Foundation evaluation handbook*. Retrieved from http://www.wkkf.org/Pubs/Tools/Evaluation/Pub770.pdf

W. K. Kellogg Foundation (January 2004). *The W. K. Kellogg Foundation logic model development guide*. Retrieved from http://www.wkkf.org/Pubs/Tools/Evaluation/Pub3669.pdf

C. Annotated bibliography and classification scheme

The annotated bibliography contains selected research and readings to which readers can refer for greater depth and detail about measuring the value of corporate philanthropy. Each selection has been classified into a category within a scheme developed to provide structure to the vast body of knowledge and literature. The categories and subcategories in the hierarchical scheme closely track and extend the flow of themes developed in the report. These selections were chosen because they represent or provide accessible reviews of important ideas within their respective subject categories. (It is impossible, of course, to create a comprehensive bibliography; many significant contributions to the field could not be included here.) For the majority of selections, web links to digital copies publicly available on the Internet are also provided.

Classification scheme page

Bibliography

1 Corporate philanthropy

The Center on Philanthropy at Indiana University (May 2007). *Corporate philanthropy: The age of integration*. Retrieved from http://www.philanthropy.iupui.edu/Research/Corporate%20giving-Target%20project%20July%202007.pdf

> The Center interviewed ten national companies recognized as leaders in corporate giving to a) examine innovation and best practices in corporate support for nonprofit organizations, b) look for emerging trends or innovative elements likely to become best practices in the next five to ten years, and c) compile information about resources that can inform companies starting corporate giving programs and/or seeking to implement best practices.

1-1 Motivations for corporate giving

Bruch, H., & Walter, F. (Fall 2005). The keys to rethinking corporate philanthropy. *MIT Sloan Management Review, 47*(1), 49-55. Retrieved from http://sloanreview.mit.edu/the-magazine/files/saleable-pdfs/47111.pdf

> The authors argue that the strategic direction of companies' philanthropic activities is often superficial and poorly controlled. One reason is a poor understanding of managerial options in this area. The supporting research (drawn from a consortium of major global companies, small and medium-sized enterprises, and an academic institution) suggests that companies' philanthropic activities rely on two perspectives: market orientation and competence orientation. The authors conclude that only philanthropic activities that create true value for the beneficiaries *and* enhance a company's business performance are sustainable in the long run.

Porter, M. E., & Kramer, M. R. (December 2002). The competitive advantage of corporate philanthropy. *Harvard Business Review, 80*(12), 56-69. Retrieved from http://www.fsg-impact.org/ideas/item/293

> The authors of this frequently cited paper argue that there is no inherent contradiction between improving competitive context and making a sincere commitment to improving society. The more closely a company's philanthropy is linked to its competitive context, the greater the company's contribution to society will be. Other potential philanthropic areas, i.e., wherein the company neither creates added value nor derives benefit, should be left to individual donors following their own charitable impulses. The paper provides a systematic framework for, and examples of, companies pursuing context-focused philanthropy.

1-2 Corporate social responsibility (CSR)

Bonini, S., Brun, N., & Rosenthal, M. (February 2009). *Valuing corporate social responsibility: McKinsey global survey results*. Retrieved from http://www.mckinseyquarterly.com/Valuing_corporate_social_responsibility_McKinsey_Global_Survey_Results_2309

> This report presents results from a field survey of 238 CFOs, investment professionals, and finance executives from a wide range of industries and regions. Most respondents believed that ESG programs create shareholder value; but neither CFOs nor professional investors fully included those considerations when evaluating business projects or companies.

Porter, M. E., & Kramer, M. R. (December 2006). Strategy and society: The link between competitive advantage and corporate social responsibility. *Harvard Business Review, 84*(12), 78-93. Retrieved from http://www.fsg-impact.org/ideas/item/435

The authors argue that companies should perceive CSR as building shared value rather than as damage-control or a PR campaign. They suggest that creating shared value should be viewed like research and development: as a long-term investment in the company's future competitiveness. Corporations are not responsible for all of the world's problems; nor do they have the resources to solve them all. But each company *can* identify the particular set of societal problems that it is best equipped to help resolve and through which it can gain the greatest competitive benefit.

Vogel, D. (2005). *The market for virtue: the potential and limits of corporate social responsibility*. Washington, DC: Brookings Institution Press.

The author provides a well-researched appraisal of the CSR movement and a critical evaluation of the business case for CSR. It is argued that CSR can be a useful tool alongside laws and regulation to bring about a significant change in corporate behavior, but cannot completely replace those laws and regulations.

1-3 Benchmarking

Committee Encouraging Corporate Philanthropy (2009). *Corporate Giving Standard: 2009 Survey Guide*. Retrieved from http://www.corporatephilanthropy.org/pdfs/benchmarking_tools/surveyguide.pdf

CECP's Survey Guide defines all terms used in the Corporate Giving Standard (CGS) Survey to ensure consistent reporting across participating companies. The in-depth research underlying the Survey Guide has helped create a common language around what it includes and excludes; it also proposes dollar valuations of in-kind goods and services. In 2009, CECP and the Taproot Foundation's Pro Bono Action Tank (PBAT) introduced standards for assigning a monetary value to pro bono services beyond the legal profession, provided by corporations to nonprofits. These standards allowed companies to track and report more accurately the value of pro bono services as a cash equivalent.

Logan, D., & Tuffrey, M. (2000). *Assessing the impact: Using the London Benchmarking Group model to assess how the community and the company benefit from corporate community involvement*. London, UK: Charities Aid Foundation.

This guide shows how companies use the LBG model to assess the impact of their corporate community involvement programs. It takes readers through the output side of the model, looking in turn at leverage, community benefit, business benefit, and impact assessment; it also provides fifteen company case studies.

Silicon Valley Community Foundation (October 2007). *Corporate philanthropy in Silicon Valley*. Retrieved from http://www.siliconvalleycf.org/docs/CorpStudy_web.pdf

This report provides an in-depth look at how businesses within a community give, the challenges and opportunities they face, and some creative approaches that other companies in the community and other regions might explore.

1-4 Case studies

Bonfiglioli, E., Moir, L., & Ambrosini, V. (2006). Developing the wider role of business in society: The experience of Microsoft in developing training and supporting employability. *Corporate Governance*, *6*(4), 401-408. Retrieved from http://www.eabis.org/index2.php?option=com_docman&gid=28&task=doc_view

This paper describes Microsoft's corporate-responsibility initiatives related to the development of employment in Europe and how these activities have created competitive advantage for Microsoft. Drawing from theories of industrial organization economics and the resource-based view of the firm, it concludes that involvement in societal projects can contribute intangible assets to the firm while also delivering social value.

Boston College Center for Corporate Citizenship and McKinsey & Company (2009). *How virtue creates value for business and society: Investigating the value of environmental, social, and governance activities.* Retrieved from http://www.bcccc.net/index.cfm?fuseaction=document.showDocumentByID&DocumentID=1269

> This study examines the relationship between ESG activities and overall value creation from a top-down perspective, by surveying CFOs, investors, and ESG professionals. It also examines the question from a bottom-up perspective, by constructing case studies of twenty companies with leading ESG programs across multiple industries. It concludes that ESG programs can create significant, quantifiable financial value. The survey results indicate agreement among CFOs, investment professionals, and ESG professionals that these programs create measurable shareholder value. The case studies of companies across industries provide an understanding of ways in which value is created.

Bzdak, M. (2007). The Johnson & Johnson bridge to employment initiative: Building sustainable community education partnerships. *Corporate Governance*, 7(4), 486-492. Retrieved from http://www.bridge2employment.org/act_sendfile.cfm?fileid=173

> This paper provides an example of a business-education partnership model—bridge to employment (BTE)—and how Johnson & Johnson engages community stakeholders to identify opportunities in the schools where company support and volunteerism can help make a difference in the lives of young community members. The Johnson & Johnson program does not train students to join its workforce, or at least not directly; instead, it looks at how to make a positive impact on students, employees, and the community at large. The paper describes how the program measures short-term student achievement as well as intermediate- and long-term outcomes, post-secondary plans, and progress as the students make their way into their chosen careers. The program is evaluated by third-party researchers and a common survey instrument is used at each site.

The Corporate Citizenship Company and Business in the Community (2006). *More than making money: Measuring the difference your company makes to society.* Retrieved from http://www.bitc.org.uk/measurement

> This report examines the concept and practicalities of measuring impact on society, by assessing the perceived drivers for measurement and conducting a review of current practice. It describes practical ways in which companies can assess the difference they make to society, from individual projects to whole company impact, and provides good practice principles, a contribution map, a toolkit of practical measures, case study examples, tips from practitioners, and a terminology guide.

1-5 Empirical studies

Lev, B., Petrovits, C., & Radhakrishnan, S. (2009). Is doing good good for you? How corporate charitable contributions enhance revenue growth. *Strategic Management Review*, forthcoming. Retrieved from http://papers.ssrn.com/sol3/papers.cfm?abstract_id=920502

> The authors examine the impact of corporate philanthropy expenditure growth on sales growth, using a large sample of charitable contributions made by U.S. public companies from 1989 through 2000. Applying Granger causality tests, they found that charitable contributions are significantly associated with future revenue, whereas the association between revenue and

future contributions is marginally significant at best. Their results were particularly pronounced for firms that are highly sensitive to consumer perception, i.e., wherein individual consumers are the predominant customers. They also documented a positive relationship between charitable contributions and customer satisfaction.

Margolis, J. D., Elfenbein, H. A., & Walsh, J. P. (2007). *Does it pay to be good? A meta-analysis and redirection of research on the relationship between corporate social and financial performance.* Retrieved from http://stakeholder.bu.edu/2007/Docs/Walsh,%20Jim%20Does%20It%20Pay%20to%20Be%20Good.pdf

> The authors conduct a meta-analysis of 192 effects from 167 scholarly studies that have investigated the empirical link between corporate social performance (CSP) and corporate financial performance (CFP). They found that the overall effect is positive but small. Across different dimensions of CSP, the association is strongest for charitable contributions, revealed misdeeds, and environmental performance; it is weakest for corporate policies and transparency. The associations are also stronger when CSP is assessed through observer perceptions and self-reported social performance than through third-party audits and mutual fund screens. The results suggested no financial penalty for CSP and as strong a link from prior CFP to subsequent CSP as the reverse. The authors concluded that future research on the link should be redirected to understand better why companies pursue CSP, the mechanisms connecting prior CFP to subsequent CSP, and how companies manage the process of pursuing both CSP and CFP simultaneously.

Sen, S., Bhattacharya, C. B., & Korschun, D. (2006). The role of corporate social responsibility in strengthening multiple stakeholder relationships: A field experiment. *Journal of the Academy of Marketing Science, 34*(2), 158-166. Retrieved from http://smgpublish.bu.edu/cb/JAMS2006.pdf

> This article presents a field study of the impact of a CSR initiative on stakeholders potentially affiliated with a company in multiple ways: as employees, customers, and investors. A substantial gift was given by a large consumer packaged-goods company to a large public university in support of an education and development center for underprivileged children in communities near the university campus. The researchers investigated whether and how awareness of this initiative affected the university students' overall beliefs and attitudes toward the firm as well as their intentions to seek employment with the firm, consume its products, and buy its stock. The study found that individuals who were aware of the CSR initiative indicated stronger company-related associations, greater organizational identification with the company, and a greater intent to purchase products, seek employment, and invest in the company. The researchers also described challenges typically confronted by field studies, such as the statistical challenge of establishing causality with sufficient control variables, how to rule out the possibility that some respondents may have been predisposed to greater awareness of CSR initiatives, and generalizing findings to other companies where stakeholders might hold different corporate associations a priori.

Wang, H., Choi, J., & Li, J. (January-February 2008). Too little or too much? Untangling the relationship between corporate philanthropy and firm financial performance. *Organization Science, 19*(1), 143-159. Retrieved from http://www.bm.ust.hk/mgmt/staff/papers/too%20little.pdf

> The authors test the relationship between corporate philanthropy expenditures and financial performance as measured by financial return on assets (ROA) and market-to-book ratios. They find that this relationship is best captured by an inverse U-shape and is stronger for firms operating in more volatile competitive environments. The research uses a panel set of corporate giving data from 817 firms listed in the Taft Corporate Giving Directory from 1987 to 1999.

2 Social impact

Colby, S. J., Stone, N., & Carttar P. (Fall 2004). Zeroing in on impact. *Stanford Social Innovation Review*, 2(2), 25-33. Retrieved from
http://www.bridgespan.org/LearningCenter/ResourceDetail.aspx?id=858
> Drawing from case studies of Larkin Street Youth Services and Harlem Children Zone, this report describes how to help an organization's decision-makers develop clarity about their intended impact and theory of change.

Neuhoff, A., & Searle, R. (Spring 2008). More bang for the buck. *Stanford Social Innovation Review*, 6(2), 33-37. Retrieved from http://www.yearup.org/marketing/SSIR.Spring2008.pdf
> This report describes the experiences of how three nonprofit organizations—Jumpstart, Teach for America, and Year Up—tracked, managed, and reduced their cost per outcome. It encouraged funders to shift their focus from cost per output to cost per outcome and to provide nonprofits with the long-term unrestricted support that will enable them to do the same.

2-1 Logic model and theory of change

Anderson, A. (October 2004). *Theory of change as a tool for strategic planning: Aspen Institute Roundtable on Community Change*. Retrieved from http://www.theoryofchange.org/pdf/tocII_final4.pdf
> This paper describes a theory-of-change approach for planning community-based initiatives. The technique and the challenges of employing it are described as lessons learned from a case study of its application during the planning phase of The Wallace Foundation Parents and Communities for Kids (PACK) initiative.

Mackinnon, A., & Arnott, N. (2008). *Grantcraft guide—Mapping change: Using a theory of change to guide planning and evaluation*. Retrieved from http://www.grantcraft.org/dl_pdf/theory_change.pdf
> This guide explains how grantmakers use theories of change to guide their questioning, unearth assumptions underlying their work, establish common language, and develop strong action plans. It also describes how a theory of change sets the stage for evaluation by clarifying goals, strategies, and milestones.

W. K. Kellogg Foundation (January 2004). *The W. K. Kellogg Foundation logic model development guide*. Retrieved from http://www.wkkf.org/Pubs/Tools/Evaluation/Pub3669.pdf
> This publication focuses on the development and use of the program logic model. The logic model and its processes facilitate thinking, planning, and communications about program objectives and actual accomplishments. This guide provides an orientation to the underlying principles and language of the program logic model so it can be used effectively in program planning, implementation, and the dissemination of results.

2-2 Outcomes measurement

McGarvey, C. (2008). *Grantcraft guide—Making measures work for you: Outcomes and evaluation*. Retrieved from http://www.grantcraft.org/dl_pdf/guide_outcome.pdf
> This guide examines tensions that drive the debate about outcomes-based measurement as well as common questions about the approach's risks and potential rewards.

University of Wisconsin-Extension (2008). *Building capacity in evaluating outcomes: A teaching and facilitating resource for community-based programs and organizations*. Madison, WI: UW-Extension, Program Development and Evaluation. Retrieved from
http://www.uwex.edu/ces/pdande/Evaluation/bceo/pdf/bceoresource.pdf

This resource provides 93 activities and materials for practitioners working with community-based programs to use in helping individuals, groups, and organizations evaluate outcomes. It provides a complete set of practical resources that can be readily used or modified when working with community-based programs. Applications in other settings are also possible.

United Way of America (2005). *Connecting program outcome measurement to community impact*. Retrieved from http://www.unitedway.org/outcomes

This report describes using program outcome measurement in the work of delivering community impact. It focuses and provides case studies on how United Way can make the most of the knowledge its agencies are gaining from this measurement.

2-2-1 Common indicators

Hatry, H., Cowan, J., Weiner, K., & Lampkin, L. (2003). *The Urban Institute Series on Outcome Management for Nonprofit Organizations: Developing community-wide outcome indicators for specific services*. Retrieved from http://www.urban.org/UploadedPDF/310813_OutcomeIndicators.pdf

This guide focuses on how local community funders and service providers can work together to develop a common core set of indicators for which each provider would regularly collect data—for its own use and to provide to funders. Even if the process does not yield a core set of indicators, convening service providers and funders to discuss outcomes measurement and identify appropriate outcome indicators seems likely to be useful. It will at least encourage some providers to improve their own outcomes-measurement efforts for internal use. However, the funders who initiate this effort must use the resulting data carefully; they can cause more harm than good if they use it exclusively to decide which programs to fund. Instead, the data should be used constructively, such as to identify best practices to disseminate among the providers or to identify programs that could be improved with additional staff training or technical assistance.

The Urban Institute and The Center for What Works (December 2006). *Building a common outcome framework to measure nonprofit performance*. Retrieved from http://www.urban.org/UploadedPDF/411404_Nonprofit_Performance.pdf

This report provides core indicators for fourteen categories of nonprofit organizations and then expands the notion of common core indicators to a much wider variety of programs by suggesting a common framework of outcome indicators for all nonprofit programs. This can provide guidance to nonprofits as they determine what and how to measure and will ease the reporting difficulties that will arise unless a common framework for outcome measurement emerges.

2-3 Evaluations

Association for the Study and Development of Community and The Robert Wood Johnson Foundation (2003). *A guide to evaluation primers*. Retrieved from http://www.rwjf.org/files/publications/RWJF_ResearchPrimer_0804.pdf

This report is an orientation guide to eleven handbooks and basic primers (introductory pieces) on program evaluation. These primers are not academic texts; they are designed for the non-expert and explain some central aspects of evaluation and why they are important. The primers also outline what the Robert Wood Johnson Foundation expects from evaluation. This is helpful to both evaluators and the grantees whose efforts might be evaluated.

The National Science Foundation Directorate for Education & Human Resources, Division of Research, Evaluation, and Communication (2002). *The 2002 user-friendly handbook for project evaluation.* Retrieved from http://www.nsf.gov/pubs/2002/nsf02057/nsf02057.pdf

> This handbook provides managers working with the National Science Foundation (NSF) with a basic guide for the evaluation of NSF's educational programs. It is aimed at people who need to learn more about both what evaluation can do and how to perform it, not those who already have a solid base of experience in the field. It discusses quantitative and qualitative evaluation methods, suggesting ways in which they can be used as complements in an evaluation strategy. Program managers will learn about the evaluation process, NSF's requirements for evaluation, how to communicate with evaluators, and how to manage the evaluation itself.

W. K. Kellogg Foundation (January 1998). *W. K. Kellogg Foundation evaluation handbook.* Retrieved from http://www.wkkf.org/Pubs/Tools/Evaluation/Pub770.pdf

> This handbook was written primarily for project directors who have direct responsibility for the ongoing evaluation of W. K. Kellogg Foundation-funded projects. It is also a resource for other project staff with evaluation responsibilities, external evaluators, and board members. It provides a framework for thinking about evaluation and outlines a blueprint for designing and conducting evaluations, either independently or with the support of an external evaluator/consultant.

2-3-1 Social services

ChildTrends, *LINKS (Lifecourse Interventions to Nurture Kids Successfully).* Retrieved from http://www.childtrends.org/links

> In a user-friendly format for policy makers, program providers, and funders, LINKS summarizes evaluations of out-of-school time programs that work (or not) to enhance children's development. This approach was built on the concept that child development is a cumulative process that begins before birth and continues into young adulthood.

Reinelt, C., Foster, P., & Sullivan, S. (August 2002). *Evaluating outcomes and impact: A scan of 55 leadership development programs.* Boston, MA: Development Guild/DDI, Inc. Retrieved from http://leadershiplearning.org/system/files/Evaluating%20Outcomes%20and%20Impacts_0.pdf

> This report provides an overview of evaluative approaches that programs are using to capture, document, and evaluate outcomes in the field of leadership development programming.

2-3-2 Arts and culture

Americans for the Arts (2007). *Arts and economic prosperity III: The economic impact of nonprofit arts and culture organizations and their audiences.* Retrieved from http://www.artsusa.org/information_services/research/services/economic_impact/default.asp

> This report demonstrates that the nonprofit arts and culture industry is also an economic driver in these communities, generating jobs, government revenue, and tourism. It documents the economic impact of the nonprofit arts and culture industry in 156 communities and regions (representing all 50 states and the District of Columbia) and used four economic measures to define economic impact: full-time equivalent jobs, resident household income, and revenue to local and state governments.

2-3-3 Advocacy

Communications Consortium Media Center (April 2004). *Guidelines for evaluating nonprofit communications efforts*. Retrieved from http://www.ppmrn.net/images/resources/Guidelines-for-Evaluating-Nonprofit-Communications-Efforts.pdf

> This working paper offers a set of guidelines that foundations and nonprofit organizations can use when designing evaluations to learn about their investments in communications strategies and the impact of those investments.

The Innovation Network (2009). *Speaking for themselves: Advocates' perspectives on evaluation*. Retrieved from http://www.innonet.org/advocacy

> This research study surveys more than 200 nonprofit advocacy staff to provide a better understanding of advocates' views on evaluation, the advocacy strategies and capacities they find effective, and current evaluation practices.

2-3-4 Environment

Cosslett, C., Buchan, D., & Smith, J. (February 2004). *Assessing the social effects of conservation on neighbouring communities*. New Zealand: Department of Conservation Technical Series. Retrieved from http://www.doc.govt.nz/upload/documents/science-and-technical/docts29.pdf

> This document presents an overview of the theory of social impact assessment and then guides the reader through a systematic process of identifying, monitoring, and responding to the effects of conservation projects on those who live and work in neighboring communities. Social and economic effects were defined and illustrated with examples from New Zealand and elsewhere. The document presents a Social Effects Management Framework: a checklist of potential effects that may result from particular actions or changes instigated by the Department. Measures to mitigate negative effects and enhance positive ones are suggested, along with possible indicators for monitoring the effectiveness of mitigation and enhancement strategies.

2-3-5 Health

McLaughlin, C., Levy, J., Noonan, K., & Rosqueta, K. (February 2009). *Lifting the burden of malaria: An investment guide for impact-driven philanthropy*. Philadelphia, PA: The Center for High Impact Philanthropy, University of Pennsylvania. Retrieved from http://www.impact.upenn.edu/our_work/Malaria-ExecutiveSummary.html

> This guide provides examples of opportunities a philanthropist can support to prevent deaths from malaria. Through several in-depth case studies, it illustrates how nonprofits produce results in a specific location and then assesses how much it costs to achieve those results. It discusses known, effective, and cost-effective approaches that philanthropists can fund to treat and prevent the disease right now. It outlines ways in which philanthropists can strengthen health systems for longer-term impact and to support innovation. It provides tips on how to set a philanthropic strategy, evaluate investment ideas, assess post-donation impact, and apply best practices.

UNICEF. *A UNICEF guide for monitoring and evaluation: Making a difference*. Retrieved from http://www.unicef.org/reseval/index.html

> This manual explains monitoring and evaluation processes and emphasizes practical suggestions. The examples used are from health services in UNICEF programming. The manual outlines UNICEF's ideals and national capacities.

2-3-6 Education

Levin, H., Belfield, C., Muennig, P., & Rouse, C. (January 2007). *The costs and benefits of an excellent education for all of America's children.* New York, NY: Columbia University, Teachers College. http://www.cbcse.org/media/download_gallery/Leeds_Report_Final_Jan2007.pdf

> This study identifies five leading interventions that have been shown to raise high school graduation rates and calculates their costs and effectiveness. It also sums the lifetime public benefits of high school graduation. These include higher tax revenues as well as lower government spending on health, crime, and welfare, but exclude private benefits, such as higher earnings. Next, it compared the costs of the interventions to the public benefits—and found that each new high school graduate would yield a public benefit of $209,000 in higher government revenues and lower government spending for an overall investment of $82,000, divided between the costs of powerful educational interventions and additional years of school attendance leading to graduation. The net economic benefit to the public purse is therefore $127,000 per student and the benefits are 2.5 times greater than the costs.

Rhodes, H. J., Noonan, K., & Rosqueta, K. (December 2008). *Pathways to student success: A guide to translating good intentions into meaningful impact.* Philadelphia, PA: The Center for High Impact Philanthropy, University of Pennsylvania. Retrieved from http://www.impact.upenn.edu/our_work/Pathways-ExecutiveSummary.html

> This guide aims to provide independent, practical advice on how to address achievement gaps in the U.S. education system through high-impact philanthropic gifts. It reviews academic research, statistics from the U.S. Department of Education's National Center on Education Statistics, policy briefs from think tanks, program evaluations, financial and performance data on nonprofits, practitioner interviews, and the insights of a diverse set of thought leaders and educators. It translates these findings into practical guidance as to which areas to target and how to get started.

Seftor, N. S., Mamun, A., & Schirm, A. (January 2009). *The impact of regular Upward Bound on postsecondary outcomes 7-9 years after scheduled high school graduation final report.* Washington, DC: Mathematica Policy Research, Inc. Retrieved from https://www.policyarchive.org/bitstream/handle/10207/15740/upwardboundoutcomes.pdf

> Upward Bound is one of the largest and longest-running federal programs designed to help disadvantaged students prepare for, enter, and succeed in college. This report provides the national evaluation's estimates of the effects of Upward Bound on postsecondary completion and also updates previous estimates of the program's effects on other postsecondary outcomes. The survey data were collected between 2003 and 2004, approximately seven-to-nine years after sample members were scheduled to graduate from high school. By comparing the study's treatment group to its control group, the evaluation estimates the value-added effect of participating in Upward Bound for eligible students who seek the opportunity.

Strive and The University of Cincinnati Center for Urban Education (2006). *Student's roadmap to success: Critical benchmarks and transition years.* Retrieved from http://www.strivetogether.org/documents/roadmap_bibliography.pdf

> This report presents a roadmap beginning with birth and progressing through childhood, adolescence, and early adulthood to conclude at the point of transition into a desired career. Along the way are important milestones or checkpoints of a youth's developmental stages, with indicators that will provide positive evidence of progress. The rationale for the goals at each benchmark is documented in the bibliography accompanying the roadmap.

2-3-7 Economic development

Fountain, R. (2008, December 22). *The economic impact of the down-payment assistance program on the U.S. economy.* Sacramento, CA: Nehemia Corporation of America. Retrieved from http://www.dpagroundswell.org/news/DrRobertFountainReport122208.pdf

> This report provides an econometric analysis of the economic impact of home purchasing and new home construction generated through the down-payment assistance provisions of the FHA 203 (b) program. Economic benefits generated as a result of down-payment assistance programs include business, financial, insurance, and other activities related to sales transactions, as well as the additional construction of new homes to meet housing demand. The economic benefits include added employment, income, and tax generation created by the home purchase activities enabled as a result of the down-payment assistance—and these benefits are distributed throughout the economy, not just to the new home owners, sellers, and builders.

2-4 Social return on investment (SROI)

Karoly, L. A. (2008). *Valuing benefits in benefit-cost studies of social programs.* Santa Monica, CA: RAND Corporation. Retrieved from http://www.rand.org/pubs/technical_reports/2008/RAND_TR643.sum.pdf

> This study assesses state-of-the-art measurement and use of shadow prices in the application of benefit-cost analysis (BCA) to social program evaluation. The study provides a review and synthesis of the social programs for which high-quality evaluations have been conducted and the subset for which BCAs have been performed.

Kilburn, M. R., & Karoly, L. A. (2008). *The economics of early childhood policy: What the dismal science has to say about investing in children.* Santa Monica, CA: RAND Corporation. Retrieved from http://www.rand.org/pubs/occasional_papers/2008/RAND_OP227.pdf

> This paper reviews the application of two economic concepts to assessing early childhood policy: human capital theory and monetary payoffs from early childhood investments.

New Economic Foundation (2008). *Measuring value: A guide to social return on investment (SROI).* Retrieved from http://www.neweconomics.org/publications/a-guide-to-social-return-on-investment

> Backed by the Cabinet Office, this guide to SROI assists nonprofit organizations and institutions demonstrate their social, economic, and environmental impact. It was designed for anyone with an interest in SROI and written primarily with the nonprofit audience in mind.

The Nonprofit Roundtable of Greater Washington and World Bank Group (2007). *Beyond charity: Recognizing return on investment.* Retrieved from http://siteresources.worldbank.org/INTCOMOUTREACH/Resources/BeyondCharity.pdf

> Working in collaboration with the World Bank Group, the Nonprofit Roundtable addressed a series of questions about the impact of nonprofits. This report describes three components of impact: societal cost-saving, multiplying impact (e.g., nonprofits leveraging funding with donated goods and services and harnessing volunteer power), and strengthening the community.

Northern Virginia Family Service (2008). *Trickle up: A case study on community benefits of workforce development*. Retrieved from www.nvfs.org/publications/trickleup.pdf

> NVFS Training Futures (TF) conducted an extensive survey of its graduates from 1996-2006 in partnership with a third-party evaluation service. This case study report describes the results reported by 120 respondents. The numbers tell a bigger story: of how community investments in vulnerable families are multiplied by successful TF graduates—and how these investments are then multiplied and returned even larger to the community, benefiting taxpayers, the regional economy, and local employers.

Richmond, B. J., Mook, L., & Quarter, J. (Summer 2003). Social accounting for nonprofits: Two models. *Nonprofit Management and Leadership, 13*(4), 308-324. Retrieved from http://www.teses.eu/upload/Social%20accounting%20for%20nonprofits_two%20models.pdf

> This article presents two models of social accounting for nonprofits: the community SROI model and the expanded value-added statement. The article also develops a process for establishing a comparative market value for non-market social outputs.

Shapiro, R. J., & Mathur, A. (December 2008). *The social and economic value of private and community foundations*. Washington, DC: The Philanthropic Collaborative. Retrieved from www.philanthropycollaborative.org/FoundationStudy.pdf

> This study analyzes and estimates the general economic or welfare benefits generated by the work of private foundations. The authors rely on contributions data collected by the Foundation Center; the data are disaggregated into categories of activity. They then draw from a vast literature on the value of specific nonprofit and public activities to estimate the economic and social value of private foundation activities: reports published by nonprofits in each of the categories, academic literature on economic and social benefits from nonprofit activities, and government analyses of public programs in many of these areas. More than ninety such studies and evaluations are reviewed; some cover a single foundation or public program and others many programs. The authors identify the appropriate category, average the results in cases of multiple evaluations, calculate a weighted average of the reported returns or benefits for each category, and estimate each category's total returns.

Tuan, M. T. (2008). *Measuring and/or estimating social value creation: Insights into eight integrated cost approaches*. Seattle, WA: Bill & Melinda Gates Foundation. Retrieved from http://www.gatesfoundation.org/learning/Pages/december-2008-measuring-estimating-social-value-creation-report-summary.aspx

> This paper analyzes eight approaches to integrating cost in measuring and/or estimating social value creation. These various approaches bring a new level of rigor and creativity to the measurement or estimation of social value. They also illustrate the host of limitations— technical and general—related to measuring and estimating social value. The implications of these possibilities and limitations serve as a reference point for those in the social sector considering whether and how to craft their own approaches to integrating cost into their social impact measurement efforts.

Weinstein, M., with Lamy, C. (2008). *Measuring success: How Robin Hood estimates the impact of grants*. New York, NY: Robin Hood Foundation. Retrieved from http://www.robinhood.org/media/169437/2009_metrics_paper.pdf

> This manuscript describes Robin Hood's methodology, which compares the poverty-fighting value of any two grants, no matter how different in purpose. Robin Hood monetizes the value of the immediate outcomes of these grants. It estimates benefit-cost ratios for comparison—for

example, the value of graduating fifty more students from high school is compared to the value of training 75 extra home health aides. These benefit-cost ratios capture Robin Hood's best estimate of the aggregate benefit to poor people, measured in part by the projected boost in future earnings, that each grant creates per dollar spent by Robin Hood.

2-4-1 Social venture investing

Acumen Fund Metrics Team (January 2007). *The best available charitable option: Acumen Fund's approach.* Retrieved from
http://www.acumenfund.org/uploads/assets/documents/BACO%20Concept%20Paper%20final_B1cNOVEM.pdf

> Acumen Fund seeks to quantify an investment's social impact and compare it to the universe of existing charitable options for that explicit social issue. Specifically, this tool informs investors as to where their philanthropic capital will be most effective by answering the question, "For each dollar invested, how much social output will this generate over the life of the investment, relative to the best available charitable option?" This methodology, called the BACO ratio (for "best available charitable option"), is a useful starting point for assessing the social impact and cost-effectiveness of each of our investments.

Clark, C., Rosenzweig, W., Long, D., & Olsen, S. (January 2004). *Double bottom line project report: Assessing social impact in double bottom line ventures. Methods catalog.* New York, NY: The Rockefeller Foundation. Retrieved from http://www.riseproject.org/DBL_Methods_Catalog.pdf

> Double bottom line (DBL) businesses are entrepreneurial ventures that strive to achieve measurable social and financial outcomes. Through in-depth interviews with funders who have attempted to document, define, and report on the non-financial performance of their activities, this report details the methods they use and how exactly each method was applied by the specific organization or fund. The analysis is based not on theory but on concrete reported experience of costs and challenges.

Olsen, S., & Galimidi, B. (April 2008). *Catalog of SROI approaches.* San Francisco, CA: Social Venture Technology Group. Retrieved from
http://svtgroup.net/sites/default/files/publication/download/SROI_approaches_0.pdf

> This report characterizes three types of impact-measurement approaches used by social venture investors: rating systems, assessment systems, and management systems. Within each type of approach are sector-specific approaches that speak to issues particular to a certain industry, geography, or type of impact, etc. There are solutions for proving impact to a social-science standard of credibility and others that rely entirely on a company self-reporting its leading impact indicators (the latter approach is much more feasibly implemented). In all, the catalog presents information on 25 approaches currently applied in privately held companies and/or nonprofit organizations that run revenue-generating businesses.

2-5 Nonprofit management

Bradach, J. L., Tierney, T. J., & Stone, N. (December 2008). Delivering on the promise of nonprofits. *Harvard Business Review, 86*(12), 88-97. Retrieved from
http://www.isae.org/sections/documents/DeliveringonthePromiseofNonprofits.pdf

> The authors provide a framework to help nonprofits demonstrate effectiveness and focus on results. This framework comprises four questions related to strategy, capital, and talent and requires that nonprofit leaders answer these questions rigorously. The authors also illustrate these ideas in practice with examples of how several nonprofit organizations confronted the inherent challenges.

Brest, P., & Harvey, H. (2008). *Money well spent*. New York, NY: Bloomberg Press.
Drawing on examples from over 100 foundations and non-profits, this book describes
components of a smart strategy that ensures meaningful philanthropic results, through:
achieving great clarity about one's philanthropic goals; specifying indicators of success before
beginning a project; designing and implementing a plan commensurate with available
resources; evidence-based understanding of the world in which the plan will operate; and
paying careful attention to milestones to determine if you are on the path to success, or if
mid-course corrections are necessary.

Chinman, M., Imm, P., & Wandersman, A. (2004). *Getting to outcomes: Promoting accountability through
methods and tools for planning, implementation and evaluation*. Santa Monica, CA: RAND Corporation.
Retrieved from http://wwwcgi.rand.org/pubs/technical_reports/TR101/
This manual describes a community-planning, implementation, and evaluation model
(organized around 10 accountability questions) to help an agency, school, or community
coalition conduct needs assessments; select best practice programs; and effectively plan,
implement, and evaluate those programs for a particular community. Although the manual
was originally developed to help communities plan and carry out programs and policies aimed
at preventing youth drug use, it may also be useful for other efforts. It received the American
Evaluation Association's Outstanding Publication Award for 2008.

2-5-1 Operating support

Grantmakers for Effective Organizations (2008). *General operating support: Assessing the impact*. Retrieved
from http://www.arizonagrantmakersforum.org/Common/Files/GEO_assessing_impact.pdf
This report demonstrates how some grantmakers are assessing the impact of general operating
support. It identifies two prevailing approaches to assessment: one that emphasizes pre-grant
assessment and one that relies more on assessment during and after the time the grant is made.

2-5-2 Capacity building

Connolly, P. (April 2007). *Deeper capacity building for greater impact: Designing a long-term initiative to
strengthen a set of nonprofit organizations*. New York, NY: TCC Group. Retrieved from
http://www.tccgrp.com/pdfs/index.php?pub=per_brief_ltcb.pdf
This report explains how funders can plan, design, implement, and evaluate a long-term
capacity-building initiative. It was written for all sizes and types of funders (including private
foundations, corporate community involvement departments, and public agencies) wanting to
pursue an initiative.

Venture Philanthropy Partners and McKinsey & Company (2001). *Effective capacity building in nonprofit
organizations*. Retrieved from
http://www.venturephilanthropypartners.org/learning/reports/capacity/full_rpt.pdf
This report presents case studies of thirteen nonprofit organizations that have engaged in
capacity-building efforts. It presents a framework for defining capacity as well as a tool for
measuring an organization's capacity level. This framework and capacity-assessment grid
provides nonprofit managers with a practical and useful way to understand and track their
own organization's capacity and then develop plans for improvement. The report also shares
lessons learned by nonprofits who have engaged in successful capacity-building efforts.

2-5-3 Organizational learning

Woodwell, W. H. (2005). *Evaluation as a pathway to learning*. Washington, DC: Grantmakers for Effective Organizations. Retrieved from http://www.geofunders.org/document.aspx?oid=a0660000003YTaRAAW

> This report presents the latest thinking about philanthropic evaluation and grantmaker effectiveness, new models of "emergent evaluation" that emphasize learning, and the connection between evaluation and knowledge-management. It also presents several brief case studies of evaluation practices at some innovative foundations.

York, P. (2003). *Learning as we go: Making evaluation work for everyone: A briefing paper for funders and nonprofits*. New York, NY: TCC Group. Retrieved from http://www.tccgrp.com/pdfs/per_brief_lawg.pdf

> This report describes a trend of funders and nonprofits shifting away from "proving something to someone else" and toward enhancing what they do so they can achieve their own mission and share success with their peers both within and outside the organization. It distinguishes between evaluation for accountability and evaluation for learning—and characterizes the latter as a collaborative approach the authors call "evaluative learning."

2-5-4 Performance management

Derryck, D., & Haider, S. (2009, April 17). *Performance dashboards: Speedometer and odometer for social enterprise*. Retrieved from http://socialenterprisefund.ca/uploads/REDF%20-%20Performance%20Dashboards.pdf

> This presentation reviews the basics of performance dashboards: Why are they useful, how are nonprofit and for-profit dashboards different, and who looks at dashboards?

Hatry, H. P., Cowan, J., & Hendricks, M. (2004). *Analyzing outcome information: Getting the most from data*. Washington, DC: The Urban Institute. Retrieved from http://www.urban.org/publications/310973.html

> This guide suggests ways to extract information from outcome data, the goal being to use the analysis involved to help improve services for clients and ensure better outcomes in the future. The analysis of quantitative data includes adding, subtracting, multiplying, dividing, and other calculations; however, it is also much more: it requires human judgment. The combination of calculations and judgment often produces the best analysis.

Kaplan, R. S. (Spring 2001). Strategic performance measurement and management in nonprofit organizations. *Nonprofit Management and Leadership, 11*(3), 353-370. Retrieved from ftp://ftp.unibocconi.it/pub/corsi/ipas/Archivio_A_A_06_07/8126/materiale_didattico/9_kaplan.pdf

> The author developed the balanced-scorecard framework for the private sector. This framework aimed to overcome deficiencies in the financial accounting model, which fails to signal changes in a company's economic value as the organization makes substantial investments (or depletes past investments) in intangible assets. Since the introduction of the balanced scorecard, companies have been able to implement new strategies rapidly and effectively, leading to dramatic performance improvements. The article describes the nonprofit sector's adoption of the approach and provides several examples of actual implementation.

Kramer, M., Parkhurst, M., & Vaidyanathan, L. (2009). *Breakthroughs in shared measurement and social impact*. Boston, MA: FSG. Retrieved from http://www.fsg-impact.org/ideas/item/breakthroughs_in_measurement.html

> The authors review how innovative organizations have developed web-based systems for reporting performance, measuring outcomes, and coordinating efforts of social enterprises within a field.

Morley, E., & Lampkin, L. M. (2004). *Using outcome information: Making data pay off*. Washington, DC: The Urban Institute. Retrieved from http://www.urban.org/publications/311040.html

> This guide offers practical advice to help other nonprofits take full advantage of outcome data. It does this by identifying a variety of ways to use the data and describing specific methods for pursuing each use. It was designed to help nonprofits cross into performance management. Nonprofit managers find outcome data most valuable after comparisons and analyses are completed and possible explanations for unexpected findings explored. Once these steps are taken, a report clearly communicating the findings should be prepared for use within the organization and then beyond—e.g., by board members, direct service personnel, clients, funders, volunteers, community members, and other nonprofit organizations providing similar services.

2-5-4-1 Foundation performance

The Center for Effective Philanthropy (2002). *Indicators of effectiveness: Understanding and improving foundation performance*. Retrieved from http://www.effectivephilanthropy.org/images/pdfs/indicatorsofeffectiveness.pdf

> This study explores the feasibility of defining and measuring foundation performance. The Center's research draws upon surveys of foundation CEOs; confidential surveys of a random sample of grantees; in-depth structured telephone interviews with foundation trustees; and analyses of IRS 990-PF tax files, foundation annual reports, and web sites. It proposes a framework of relatively simple data collection and measurement by which any foundation can begin to monitor and improve its performance.

The Pew Charitable Trusts (2001). *Returning results: Planning and evaluation at The Pew Charitable Trusts*. Retrieved from http://www.pewtrusts.org/uploadedFiles/wwwpewtrustsorg/Reports/Miscellaneous/returning_results.pdf

> This document describes the system of determining and evaluating philanthropic investments used at The Pew Charitable Trusts. Its purpose is to share this developed approach to guide decisions about this vital aspect of the foundation's work.

2-5-5 Assessing charitable organizations

Working Group for Effective Social Investing (2008). *Guide to effective social investing*. Retrieved from http://www.alleffective.org/docs/Guide%20to%20Effective%20Social%20Investing%20102108.pdf

> Assuming the likelihood that an organization's programs deliver services of measurable social value, this report describes the development of an assessment instrument that uses clear, easily applied, and meaningful metrics to calculate the potential risk and value of an investment in a nonprofit organization.

World Economic Forum (2003). *Philanthropy measures up*. Retrieved from
http://www.salesforcefoundation.org/files/Philanthropy+Measures+Up.pdf

> This report was written from the perspective of a grantmaking body to provide philanthropists, foundations, and corporations wishing to improve their impact-measurement with the practical tools to do so. It provides summaries of fieldwork and presents practical tools and findings to assist philanthropists in their quest to understand the impact of their charitable efforts.

2-5-5-1 Grants management

Idealware (January 2008). *Grants management software: Survey results and analysis*. Retrieved from
http://www.idealware.org/gm_survey.php

> This report presents the findings of an online survey of grantmaking organizations asked about the software they use to manage their grants. The survey asked respondents demographic and software-specific questions as well as questions rating the importance and effectiveness of their software at handling a list of thirty grants-management attributes. The raw survey findings were subsequently folded into another report, *Consumers' guide to grants management software*, which provides a larger audience with an overview of available software, important features, and how those features compare across the software.

3 Business benefits

Australian Government Department of Families, Housing, Community Services and Indigenous Affairs. *Corporate community involvement—Establishing a business case*. Retrieved from
http://www.fahcsia.gov.au/sa/communities/progserv/documents/cci_report_07/default.htm

> This study assembles the views of 115 large Australian companies on current attitudes and commitment to community involvement. It explores these companies' programs, motives for community involvement, anticipated outcomes, and potential directions.

The Council on Foundations and Walker Information (October 2000). *Measuring the business value of corporate philanthropy*. Retrieved from
http://classic.cof.org/members/content.cfm?itemnumber=761&navItemNumber=2409

> This text describes the development of a survey-based measurement tool that could demonstrate a tangible link between corporate philanthropy and business success. The tool would equip an individual company to demonstrate the link between stakeholder perceptions of company giving and the intentions of those stakeholders to behave in ways that directly affect business success.

McElhaney, K. (Fall 2008). Measuring what matters? Evaluating CSR's return on investment. *Leading Perspectives*, BSR Conferences 2008 Special Issue, 10-17. Retrieved from
http://www.bsr.org/research/leading-perspectives.cfm

> The author argues that, using a lack of ROI quantification as an excuse, the CSR community may not be committing adequate resources to CSR strategy development and execution. Instead of focusing on finding the exact ROI of CSR using traditional methods, the author recommends that companies measure value using other more useful metrics. The author asserts that, just like many other business factors, CSR's ROI can be measured, if perhaps not as precisely as we would like.

Weber, M. (2008). The business case for corporate social responsibility: A company-level measurement approach for CSR. *European Management Journal, 26*, 247-261.

This paper focuses on how to measure the business impact of CSR activities from a company perspective. It develops a multi-step conceptual measurement model that allows managers to evaluate their company-specific business case for CSR. A case example illustrates how to apply the model.

3-1 Employee engagement

Bhattacharya, C. B., Sen S., & Korschun, D. (Winter 2008). Using corporate social responsibility to win the war for talent. *MIT Sloan Management Review, 49*(2), 37-44. Retrieved from http://sloanreview.mit.edu/the-magazine/files/saleable-pdfs/49215.pdf

The authors summarize findings from their research program to understand better how, when, and why employees react to a firm's corporate citizenship initiatives. Producing the report involved in-depth interviews; focus groups; a large global survey with employees of a major consumer-goods company; and a series of interviews and online surveys of employees from ten other companies in the manufacturing, retail, and service sectors. The research indicates that corporate citizenship activities provide an opportunity to serve as an effective internal marketing lever. And yet: there is great divergence in how such activities are implemented and therefore in how effective they are in managing talent. Companies need to segment employees based on the relative importance of those employees' corporate citizenship-related needs and then design and target segment-specific programs to meet those diverse needs. Successful strategies tend to be co-created with employees to satisfy varying desires and encourage employee identification.

Caldwell, M. (2008). Uncovering the hidden value in corporate social responsibility. *Synnovation, 3*(1), 68-75. Retrieved from http://www.towersperrin.com/tp/getwebcachedoc?webc=USA/2008/200807/Uncovering_the_H idden_Value_in_Corporate_Social_Responsibility.pdf

The author notes that a key differentiator of companies with superior financial performance is an engaged workforce. Towers Perrin's 2007 Global Workforce Study revealed that an organization's reputation for social responsibility is one of the top ten drivers of employee engagement worldwide. Corporate responsibility also plays a role as a driver of employee retention, along with the organization's reputation as a great place to work. Employee volunteer programs can be effective in giving employees: (1) a sense of program ownership and control, (2) a sense of individual participation and contribution, (3) more immediate feedback on results, and (4) the opportunity to experience firsthand a real awareness of positive change for the effort expended. One of the bonus benefits of volunteerism for employees and organizations alike is the opportunity for individuals to polish and display management skills away from the office, in a somewhat less threatening environment. Companies need periodically to survey for two key pieces of information: (1) How familiar are employees with the details of the company's various corporate citizenship-volunteer programs? and (2) What is their perception—positive or negative—of the programs' societal value?

Jones, D. A. (2007). *Employee treatment and the engaged workforce: Reciprocation and organizational identification*. Retrieved from http://www.uvm.edu/~sustnbus/readings/Reciprocation_and_Organizational_Identification_Proc esses.pdf

> The author reviews two research literatures—organizational identification and social exchange (reciprocation)—that provide managers with effective tools for treating employees well and reaping benefits via the employees' response. "Employee relations" is often considered an integral part of corporate responsibility, relevant for understanding how corporate-responsibility initiatives directed at external stakeholders (e.g., community-focused programs and environmental initiatives) can be leveraged as part of human resource management strategy. Organizational identification refers to an employee's feeling of "oneness" with his or her organization. Employees who identify strongly with their organization experience its successes and failures as their own and are motivated to foster positive identities by engaging in behaviors that help achieve organizational goals. Doing so reflects positively on the organization and, by association, on themselves. Socially responsible business practices are likely to invoke organizational identification processes among employees. Another dominant paradigm for understanding employment relationships is social exchange and reciprocity. Many studies show that employees who receive favorable treatment from their managers and organization respond through greater commitment and loyalty and by performing behaviors that benefit their managers and organization.

Tuffrey, M. (2003). *Good companies, better employees—How community involvement and good corporate citizenship can enhance employee morale, motivation, commitment and performance*. London, UK: The Corporate Citizenship Company. Retrieved from http://www.centrica.com/files/reports/2005cr/files/csr_Good_companies_better_employees.pdf

> This report explores how corporate community involvement and wider corporate citizenship contribute to business success by enhancing employee morale, motivation, commitment, and performance. It comprises a new general survey of attitudes among employees in the U.K., more specific surveys of attitudes within the participating companies, and a case study seeking to track impact down to the bottom line, etc.

3-1-1 Human resource management

Charlton, K., & Osterweil, C. (Fall 2005). Measuring return on investment in executive education: A quest to meet client needs or pursuit of the holy grail? *The Ashridge Journal*, 6-13. Retrieved from http://www.ashridge.org.uk/Website/Content.nsf/FileLibrary/FC30125A4420D12B80257602003 9C093/$file/MeasuringROI.pdf

> The authors survey HR professionals and senior executive sponsors to understand better the demands for proof of financial ROI on executive education programs. Their paper suggests that people may mean different things when they talk about ROI and that sponsors may not be as wedded to proof of financial ROI as many HR professionals assume.

Edmans, A. (2008, December 30). *Does the stock market fully value intangibles? Employee satisfaction and equity prices*. Retrieved from http://papers.ssrn.com/sol3/papers.cfm?abstract_id=985735

> The author analyzes the relationship between employee satisfaction and long-run stock returns. A portfolio of the "100 Best Companies to Work for in America" earned an annualized excess return of 4% from 1984-2005. Returns were even more significant in the 1998-2005 sub-period. The list was widely publicized by *Fortune* magazine; still, it was

surprising that the Best Companies also exhibited significantly more positive earnings and returns. The author suggests these findings have three main implications. First, employee satisfaction is positively correlated with shareholder returns and need not represent excessive non-pecuniary compensation. Second, the stock market does not fully value intangibles, even when independently verified by a publicly available and widely disseminated survey. Third, certain socially responsible investing screens may improve investment returns.

Faleye, O., & Trahan, E. (May 2006). *Is what's best for employees best for shareholders?* Retrieved from http://papers.ssrn.com/sol3/papers.cfm?abstract_id=888180

The authors study the effect of labor-friendly corporate practices on shareholder outcomes using firms selected by *Fortune* magazine as the "100 Best Companies to Work for in America" over 1998-2004. They find that investors react positively to the list's announcement and that list firms subsequently outperform a size- and industry-matched control group on productivity, profitability, and value creation. They interpret the results to be consistent with the hypothesis that genuine management concern for employees translates into higher productivity and profitability, which in turn facilitate value creation. The benefits of creating an employee-friendly environment significantly outweigh the costs, assert the authors; what is best for employees is (at least) good for shareholders.

Weibel, A., Rost, K., & Osterloh, M. (2007). *Crowding-out of intrinsic motivation—Opening the black box*. Retrieved from http://papers.ssrn.com/sol3/papers.cfm?abstract_id=957770

While standard economics state that pay-for-performance increases work efforts, psychological economics counter that it sometimes weakens work efforts. The authors conduct a meta-analysis and a case study and show both predictions are valid in a job-related environment. Performance-contingent pay strengthens extrinsic motivation; simultaneously, performance-contingent pay weakens intrinsic motivation, i.e., provokes a motivation-crowding-out effect. The authors conclude that pay-for-performance produces hidden costs of rewards.

3-1-2 Employee volunteer programs

Bartel, C. A. (2001). Social comparisons in boundary-spanning work: Effects of community outreach on members' organizational identity and identification. *Administrative Science Quarterly, 46,* 379-413. Abstract retrieved from http://psycnet.apa.org/?fa=main.doiLanding&uid= 2002-00350-001

The author conducts a field evaluation of the experience of employees who participated in community-outreach programs for The Pillsbury Company. The study involves a multi-method panel design and collected survey, interview, and observational data from participants and their supervisors during several time periods. The author begins by posing survey questions to employees (their sense of collective self-esteem and identification with their company) and their supervisors (their assessment of employees' work behaviors) both before and after the employees participated in the company's community-outreach program. To form a control group, supervisors were also asked to evaluate a group of non-participants. Comparing differences in pre- and post-program survey reports, the author finds that participation enhances the collective self-esteem of employees felt for their company. In turn, those employees who feel that these needs are fulfilled also perceive a stronger level of identification with the company. For employees whose organizational identification has become stronger, their supervisors report higher interpersonal co-operation and work-related effort.

Center for Corporate Citizenship at Boston College and Points of Light Foundation (2005, June 21). *Measuring employee volunteer programs: The human resources model.* Retrieved from http://www.bcccc.net/index.cfm?fuseaction=document.showDocumentByID&DocumentID=836

This report documents the findings from a joint research project conducted by The Center for Corporate Citizenship at Boston College and the Points of Light Foundation. The project examined the value-added benefits of employee volunteering based on interviews with five companies. The report identifies four HR goals and suggests metrics and measurement methods:

1. Recruitment: Are candidates more likely to accept a position because of the program? Include standardized questions during HR interview or new-employee orientation process to assess if potential employees cite this reason.
2. Retention: a) Do employees who participate in the program stay longer? Track administrative data on length of employment and participation. b) Are employees who participate more loyal than those who do not? Survey a random sample of participants and non-participants on perceptions of loyalty and commitment to company.
3. Skills development: Has participant leadership potential been enhanced? Include questions on supervisor evaluations to determine leadership ability of participants and non-participants.
4. Morale building: Do participating employees feel more connected to colleagues and rate their work/life balance higher than non-participants do? Survey a random sample of participants and non-participants on their perceptions of connectedness and work/life balance.

Hills, G., & Mahmud, A. (September 2007). *Volunteering for impact: Best practices in international corporate volunteering.* Boston, MA: FSG. Retrieved from http://www.fsg-impact.org/ideas/item/536

A compilation of best practices in international corporate volunteering (ICV), this study examines ICV within two principal models: local service, in which employees based in countries outside headquarters volunteer in local communities, and cross-border service, in which employees travel abroad to volunteer. Through interviews and the analysis of ICV programs at fourteen multinational corporations, the authors detail current programs and make recommendations to guide corporate philanthropy executives and ICV program managers to build high-impact volunteer programs.

Peterson, Dane K. (2004). Benefits of participation in corporate volunteer programs: employees' perceptions. *Personnel Review, 33*(5-6), 615-627.

This study investigates the benefits associated with corporate volunteer programs. The authors conducted a mail survey of business professionals randomly drawn from a computerized list of alumni from a large Midwestern American state university. The results demonstrated that employees view volunteerism as an effective means of developing or enhancing job-related skills. This was particularly true for female employees and employees participating in a formal volunteer program. Organizational commitment was also higher for volunteers from companies with a corporate volunteer program than for non-volunteers with organizations without a corporate volunteer program.

Vian, T., Feeley, M., Macleod, W., Richards, S., & McCoy, K. (2007, September 21). *Measuring the impact of international corporate volunteering: Lessons learned from the Global Health Fellows Program of Pfizer Corporation: Final Report.* Boston, MA: Center for International Health, Boston University School of Public Health. Retrieved from http://media.pfizer.com/files/philanthropy/bu_icv_report_9_21_07.pdf

> The authors research and develop tools and methods for evaluating international corporate volunteer (ICV) service programs. They use empirical data from the Pfizer Global Health Fellows (GHF) Program from October 2006 through May 2007. The goal of the study was to design a toolkit to measure the impact of ICV on recipient organizations and their ability to deliver efficient, high-quality services. The authors pilot-test the evaluation tools with a small sample of Pfizer corporate volunteers.

3-1-3 Recruitment

Greening, D. W., & Turban, D. B. (September 2000). Corporate social performance as a competitive advantage in attracting a quality workforce. *Business and Society, 39*(3), 254-280.

> The authors hypothesize that firms can use corporate social performance activities to attract job applications. They conduct an experiment in which they manipulated information about corporate social performance and find that prospective job applicants are more likely to pursue jobs from socially responsible firms than from firms with poor reputations.

Montgomery, D. B., & Ramus, C. A. (December 2007). *Including corporate social responsibility, environmental sustainability, and ethics in calibrating MBA job preferences.* Retrieved from http://papers.ssrn.com/sol3/papers.cfm?abstract_id=412124

> The authors calibrate the relative importance of a wide variety of job factors on MBA job preferences, using the conjoint calibration survey method used by marketing scientists. Their survey sample comprises 759 MBAs graduating from eleven business schools (8 in North America and 3 in Europe). Based on their findings, the fourteen job factors ranked in declining relative importance were: Intellectual Challenge, Geographic Area, Financial Package, Ethical Reputation, Caring about Employees, People in Organization, Learning on Job, Type of Position, Advancement, Dynamics & Culture, Business Travel, Environmental Sustainability, Community-Stakeholder Relations, and Economic Sustainability. The authors also asked each respondent how much salary he or she would be willing to give up in order to work for a company that: (1) cares about employees, (2) cares about stakeholders such as the community, (3) commits to environment sustainability, (4) is ethical in its business practices, and (5) exhibits all four of these qualities. The MBAs on average were willing to forego 8.6% of their expected income in order to work for an organization that cares about its employees and overall were willing to forego 14.4% of their mean expected income to work for an organization exhibiting all four characteristics of social responsibility.

Turban, D. B., & Greening, D. W. (June 1997). Corporate social performance and organizational attractiveness to prospective employers. *Academy of Management Journal, 40*(3), 658-672.

> The authors find that companies' corporate social performance is related positively to their reputations and to their attractiveness as employers. The results are based on responses from students in a senior-level strategic management class asked to rate each of 189 companies in terms of its attractiveness as an employer. A different set of students rated the companies in terms of their reputations, while ratings of social performance came from analysts from the independent research company, KLD.

3-2 Customer loyalty

Bhattacharya, C. B., & Sen, S. (Fall 2004). Doing better at doing good: When, why and how consumers respond to corporate social initiatives. *California Management Review, 47*(1), 9-24. Retrieved from http://smgpublish.bu.edu/cb/CMR2004.pdf

> Marketplace polls suggest that a positive relationship exists between a company's CSR actions and consumers' reactions to that company and its products. The authors' research, which uses a variety of methodologies such as focus groups, in-depth interviews, surveys, and experiments, shows that consumer reactions to CSR are not as straightforward and evident as the marketplace polls suggest. There are numerous factors that affect whether a firm's CSR activities translate into consumer purchases. The authors propose a framework to help managers understand how and why consumers' respond to CSR initiatives and develop optimal CSR strategies. They argue that, from a consumer perspective of CSR initiatives, "one size does not fit all." Companies also need to consider not only external outcomes such as purchase and loyalty, but also internal changes, such as consumer awareness, attitudes, and attributions about why companies are engaging in CSR activities.

Smith, V., & Langford, P. (2009). Evaluating the impact of corporate social responsibility programs on consumers. *Journal of Management & Organization, 15*, 97-109.

> This paper critically reviews the empirical and theoretical literature relating to CSR programs and highlights ways in which CSR can have a positive effect on consumer attitudes and behaviors. The paper also identifies a number of consumer- and company-specific factors that moderate the impact of CSR on consumers, e.g., CSR initiatives can decrease consumer purchase intentions if many consumers believe that the CSR is being carried out at the expense of corporate ability or product quality. The paper concludes that companies need to understand both their consumers and their companies' performance according to a range of traditional standards in order to implement CSR effectively.

3-2-1 Marketing management

Keiningham, T. L., Cooil, B., Aksoy, L., Andreassen, T. W., & Weiner, J. (2007). The value of different customer satisfaction and loyalty metrics in predicting customer retention, recommendation, and share-of-wallet. *Managing Service Quality, 17*(4), 361-384.

> This research examines different customer satisfaction and loyalty metrics and tests their relationship to customer retention, recommendation, and share-of-wallet using micro-level (i.e., individual customer) data. The data for this study came from a two-year longitudinal Internet panel of more than 8,000 American customers of firms in one of three industries (retail banking, mass-merchant retail, and Internet service providers (ISPs)). The results indicated that intention-to-recommend alone does not suffice as a single predictor of customers' future loyalty behavior. Use of a multiple-indicator rather than a single-predictor model performed better in predicting customer recommendations and retention.

3-2-2 Cause-related marketing

Cone (2008). *Past. Present. Future. The 25th anniversary of cause marketing.* Retrieved from http://www.coneinc.com/news/request.php?id=1187

> This report surveys the landscape on trends and potential business returns of cause initiatives. It discusses key cause-related milestones of the last 25 years (including the 2008 Cone Cause Evolution Study and the 2008 Cone/Duke University Behavioral Cause Study) and highlights marketing insights into the "socially responsible consumer."

Hoeffler, S., & Keller, K. L. (Spring 2002). Building brand equity through corporate societal marketing. *Journal of Public Policy & Marketing, 21*(1), 78-89. Retrieved from http://public.kenan-flagler.unc.edu/courses/mba/mba260e/Hoeffler_JPPM.pdf

> The authors review six means by which cause-related marketing programs can build brand equity: (1) building brand awareness, (2) enhancing brand image, (3) establishing brand credibility, (4) evoking brand feelings, (5) creating a sense of brand community, and (6) eliciting brand engagement. The authors also address three key questions revolving around how programs achieve their effects, which cause or causes a firm should choose, and how programs should be branded. The authors offer a series of research propositions and conclude by outlining a set of potential future research directions.

3-3 Reputation

Boston College Center for Corporate Citizenship and the Reputation Institute (2009). *Building reputation here, there and everywhere: Worldwide views on local impact of corporate responsibility.* Retrieved from http://www.bcccc.net/index.cfm?fuseaction=Document.showDocumentById&documentId=1270

> The Reputation Institute's Pulse measure identifies several different dimensions of a company's activity that relate to its reputation and provides a summary indicator of reputation overall. The 2008 Global Pulse Report survey of the public suggests that the top reputation driver is product and service ratings. The next highest drivers are perceptions of a company's citizenship, governance, and workplace practices—affirming that CSR, too, influences reputation. This research report sums the ratings of citizenship, governance, and workplace quality to create a CSR Index and provides an analysis of how the public rates 600 global companies in 27 countries on the CSR Index.

Fombrun, C. J., Gardberg, N. A., & Barnett, M. L. (2000). Opportunity platforms and safety nets: Corporate citizenship and reputational risk. *Business and Society Review, 105*(1), 85-106. Retrieved from http://www.www.reputationinstitute.com/press/fombrunetal2002.pdf

> The authors argue that corporate social performance (CSP) activities do not directly impact the company's financial performance, but instead affect the bottom line via its stock of reputational capital, the financial value of its intangible assets. They describe examples supporting the view of corporate citizenship as a strategic business tool with two dimensions. One, corporate citizenship helps integrate companies into the social fabric of local communities and mitigates the risk of reputational losses that can result from alienating key stakeholders. Two, corporate citizenship also helps a company generate reputational gains that improve a company's ability to attract resources, enhance performance, and build competitive advantage.

Godfrey, P. C., Merrill C. B., & Hansen, J. M. (2009). The relationship between corporate social responsibility and shareholder value: An empirical test of the risk management hypothesis. *Strategic Management Journal, 30*, 425-445. Abstract retrieved from http://rmrr.com/pdf/Godfrey—Corporate%20Social%20Responsibility%20and%20Shareholder%20Value.pdf

> The authors examine how a company's CSR activities are linked to shareholder value when the company suffers a negative reputation event. They posit that such activities create goodwill that lead stakeholders to temper negative judgments and sanctions of companies. They perform an event study of 178 negative legal/regulatory actions against companies from 1993-2003 and find that participation in institutional CSR activities—those aimed at a firm's secondary stakeholders, such as society at large—provides an "insurance-like" benefit, while participation in technical CSRs—activities targeting trading partners—yields no such benefits.

3-3-1 Reputational risk management

Eccles, R. G., Newquist, S. C., & Schatz, R. (February 2007). Reputation and its risks. *Harvard Business Review, 85*(22), 104-114. Retrieved from http://annenberg.usc.edu/images/pdfs/current/hbr.jan2007-reputation-article.pdf

> The authors note that companies tend to focus energies on handling reputational threats already surfaced. However, this is crisis management—a reactive approach to limit damage—not risk management. The authors provide a framework and examples for proactively managing reputational risks and explain the factors that affect risk levels and how a company can quantify and control them. They suggest that managing reputational risk is not an extraordinarily expensive undertaking that will require years to implement. At most well-managed companies, many of the elements are already in place, just disparately. The additional costs of installing and using the new tools described in their article to identify risks and design responses are modest compared with the value at stake for many companies.

3-4 Business innovation

Holmes, S., & Moir, L. (2007). Developing a conceptual framework to identify corporate innovations through engagement with nonprofit stakeholders. *Corporate Governance, 7*(4), 414-422. Retrieved from http://www.eabis.org/index2.php?option=com_docman&gid=9&task=doc_view

> The authors identify the pressure on companies to position themselves as responsible corporate citizens as a key driver of the increase in collaborative relationships between corporations and nonprofit organizations—with innovation and learning recognized as benefits the firms are likely to derive from such relationships. The authors examine factors that can foster or impede the identification and development of firm-related innovations that result from engagement with nonprofit stakeholders and develop a framework for analyzing how business-nonprofit relations generate innovation outcomes.

Nelson, J., & Jenkins, B. (2006). *Investing in social innovation: Harnessing the potential of partnership between corporations and social entrepreneurs (Corporate Social Responsibility Initiative working paper no. 20)*. Cambridge, MA: Harvard University John F. Kennedy School of Government. Retrieved from http://www.ksg.harvard.edu/m-rcbg/CSRI/publications/workingpaper_20_nelson_jenkins.pdf

> This paper examines some of the innovative alliances that already exist between corporate leaders and social entrepreneurs in both developed and developing countries. It suggests a conceptual framework for thinking about the different ways through which companies can support social entrepreneurship. The authors outline the business case for how such alliances can help companies meet their business goals and support their corporate values.

3-4-1 Financial valuation models

Damodaran, A. (January 2006). *Dealing with intangibles: Valuing brand names, flexibility and patents*. Retrieved from http://www.stern.nyu.edu/~adamodar/pdfiles/papers/intangibles.pdf

> The author critiques standard valuation models such as discounted cash-flow models, which fail to account fully for the many intangible assets possessed by firms. There have been attempts to value brand name, patents, trademarks, and copyrights and bring them to the balance sheet. The author would expand this list to consider the flexibility a firm may preserve to expand its market or enter new ones. The paper considers a variety of ways in which these assets can be valued and outlines the consequences for investors.

4 Investor influence

Landier, A., & Nair, V. B. (2009). *Investing for change: Profit from responsible investment*. Oxford, UK: Oxford University Press.

> The authors present a wide range of research and statistics to make the argument for individuals adding socially responsible investments to their portfolios. They divide investors into three stylized color categories based on value beliefs and how much they are willing to pay for corroborative investments. "Yellow" investors feel morally obliged to avoid companies that are incompatible with one or more of their values; doing otherwise, they believe, would be immoral. "Red" investors are at the other end of the SRI spectrum: not motivated by moral concerns. Instead, they will not tolerate investment strategies that negatively impact financial performance in any way. "Blue" investors are pragmatic: only interested in being responsible investors if they are convinced it can change the world in the direction of their values and that the financial cost is small.

4-1 Socially responsible investing (SRI)

Robinson, M. J., Kleffner, A., & Bertels, S. (2009). *The value of reputation for corporate social responsibility: Empirical evidence*. Retrieved from http://www.northernfinance.org/2008/papers/221.pdf

> The authors conduct an event study over the period 2002-2007 and find that there is a permanent positive stock market reaction to the addition of a firm to the DJSI; however, there is not a significant loss in value to firms as a result of their removal from the DJSI. These findings suggest that being included in this index is very valuable for a firm; it has been shown to result in a market value increase of almost 4%.

Statman, M., & Glushkov, D. (2009). The wages of social responsibility. *Financial Analysts Journal*, forthcoming. Retrieved from http://papers.ssrn.com/sol3/papers.cfm?abstract_id=1372848

> The authors analyze 1992-2007 returns of stocks rated on social responsibility by KLD and find that this tilt gave socially responsible investors a return advantage relative to that of conventional investors. However, socially responsible investors typically shun stocks associated with tobacco, alcohol, gambling, firearms, the military, and nuclear operations. This behavior brought to the socially responsible investors a return disadvantage relative to conventional investors. The return advantage of tilts toward stocks of companies with high social responsibility scores is largely offset by the return disadvantage that comes from the exclusion of stocks with "shunned" companies. The return of the DS 400 Index of socially responsible companies was approximately equal to that of the S&P 500® Index of conventional companies.

4-1-1 Environmental, social, and governance (ESG) reporting

The Asset Management Working Group of the United Nations Environment Programme Finance Initiative and Mercer (October 2007). *Demystifying responsible investment performance: A review of key academic and broker research on ESG factors*. Retrieved from http://www.unepfi.org/fileadmin/documents/Demystifying_Responsible_Investment_Performance_01.pdf

> This report aims to capture the current state and direction of research in how to incorporate ESG issues into investment and decision-making processes: the first principle of the United Nations Principles for Responsible Investment (PRI). It reviews a diverse set of academic and broker studies that analyze responsible investment performance at both the company/stock and fund/portfolio level, as well as the materiality of ESG factors.

CFA Institute Centre for Financial Market Integrity (May 2008). *Environmental, social, and governance factors at listed companies: A manual for investors*. Retrieved from http://www.cfapubs.org/doi/pdf/10.2469/ccb.v2008.n2.1

> This manual aims to help investment professionals identify and properly evaluate the risks and opportunities ESG issues present for investors in public companies. Increasingly, analysts are probing a wide variety of non-financial factors to understand better their potential impact on a company's valuation. Traditional financial analysis already accounts for certain "intangibles" (such as goodwill), but ESG factors represent a broad set of dynamic, non-financial attributes that may ultimately affect investment valuation. This manual clarifies the broad range of ESG factors to be considered as part of a proper analysis of companies; it also indicates where one can find this information and provides a primer on the diverse vocabulary of ESG analysis.

Enhanced Analytics Initiative (June 2008). *A steady course in rough seas: Evaluation of extra-financial research*. Retrieved from http://www.enhancedanalytics.com/portal/Library/Documents/EAI/EVALUATION/en_LIB04175.pdf

> The Enhanced Analytics Initiative (EAI) is an international collaboration between asset owners and asset managers aimed at encouraging better investment research, in particular research that takes account of the impact of extra-financial issues on long-term investment. The Initiative incentivizes research providers to compile better and more detailed analysis of extra-financial issues within mainstream research. The report covers research produced by 22 providers in the period of November 2007-April 2008. EAI members reward research providers that are effective in analyzing long-term trends and material extra-financial issues (EFIs) and intangibles.

Lydenberg, S., & Grace, K. (November 2008). *Innovations in social and environmental disclosure outside the United States*. Retrieved from http://www.domini.com/common/pdf/Innovations_in_Disclosure.pdf

> This background paper highlights various noteworthy developments worldwide on environmental and social reporting requirements by regulatory bodies and stock exchanges. The initiatives in the five case studies—Brazil, France, Malaysia, South Africa, and Sweden—provide models for similar regulatory action by U.S. agencies or stock exchanges to promote transparency and efficiency in American markets.

Welsh, H. (May 2008). *2008 ESG background report: Sustainability reporting*. New York, NY: RiskMetrics Group. Retrieved from http://www.riskmetrics.com/docs/2008_ESG_sustainability

> This report provides a review of recent sustainability reporting trends, including American shareholder engagement in 2008, the demand for and extent of corporate sustainability reporting, and the Global Reporting Initiative.

4-1-2 Social ratings

Dow Jones Sustainability Indexes (September 2009). *Dow Jones Sustainability World Index Guide, Version 11.1*. Retrieved from http://www.sustainability-index.com/djsi_pdf/publications/Guidebooks/DJSI_Guidebook_World_80.pdf

> This guidebook describes the underlying Corporate Sustainability Assessment, index features and data dissemination, periodic review and ongoing review, the calculation model, and management responsibilities for the Dow Jones Sustainability Indexes (DJSI).

KLD Research and Analytics (2007). *Environmental, social, and governance ratings criteria. SOCRATES: The corporate social ratings monitor.* Retrieved from
http://www.kld.com/research/ratings_indicators.html

> This report summarizes research into the ESG performance and controversial business involvement (CBI) performance of listed companies since 1988. Their research is used by money managers, investment advisors, academics, NGOs and media institutions. The report lists ratings and definitions for issues covered by KLD in their SOCRATES research database. ESG criteria measure corporate social responsibility across a range of issues that impact a company's various stakeholders. CBI criteria measure a company's level of involvement in industries such as gambling and tobacco.

4-2 Responsible investing (RI)

UNEP Finance Initiative (2008). *PRI Report on Progress.* Retrieved from
http://www.unpri.org/report08/

> The United Nations Principles for Responsible Investment initiative was launched in 2006. This is the second annual report assessing PRI implementation by signatories and it summarizes progress made and the impact that the initiative is having on the market—by gaining new signatories, assisting signatories in implementing the principles, and fostering greater collaboration among signatories in doing so. The number of signatories has grown to approximately 360 institutions, representing over $14 trillion in assets.

4-2-1 Sustainability

Kiernan, M. (2008). *Investing in a sustainable world: Why GREEN is the new color of money on Wall Street.* New York, NY: AMACOM.

> This book introduces trends in the new sustainable investment strategies and in how mainstream asset owners, pension funds, foundations and endowments, and sovereign wealth funds are actively incorporating ESG factors into their investment strategies. It also examines some of the pioneering money managers, consultants, and research firms driving this field.

UN Global Compact and UNEP Finance Initiatives (2003). *Mainstreaming sustainable investment: Summary report.* Retrieved from
http://www.unepfi.org/fileadmin/documents/investors_global_compact_report_2003.pdf

> This report summarizes the proceedings of a workshop organized by the United Nations Global Compact and UNEP Finance Initiatives in Washington, D.C. on September 17, 2003. The workshop convened a group of leading authorities from the finance and industrial sectors to initiate a conversation on the issue of sustainable investment initiatives and strategies for integrating sustainable investment into the mainstream financial community. The group included representatives from sell-side SRI research, investor relations departments, rating agencies, institutional investors, NGOs, SRI networks, and portfolio managers.

D. Acknowledgements

CECP acknowledges and thanks the following leading practitioners and experts who served on our panel of external reviewers and provided many helpful comments on our report or generously gave constructive interviews that significantly informed our analysis.

Interview List

Curtis Ravenal
Bloomberg L.P.

Debra Natenshon
The Center for What Works

David Vidal
The Conference Board

Kris Taylor
Ecolab Inc.

Lucien Chan
Bobbi Silten
Gap Inc.

Bob Corcoran
Kelli Wells
General Electric Company

Mary Jane Melendez
General Mills, Inc.

Jeff Sturchio
Global Health Council

Dina Powell
Goldman, Sachs & Co.

Stan Litow
IBM

Joan Trant
International Association of
Microfinance Investors

Sharon D'Agostino
Brittany Hume
Joy Marini
Rick Martinez
Johnson & Johnson

Sheila Bonini
Laura Callanan
McKinsey & Company

Kristy Becerra
Fran Lasserson
Moody's Corporation

Joe Kelsch
Troy Stremler
Newdea, Inc.

Steve Morgan
Pfizer Inc

Jennifer Arrowsmith
Allison Kelly
QUALCOMM Incorporated

Cynthia Exposito Lamy
Michael Weinstein
Robin Hood Foundation

Margot Brandenburg
Rockefeller Foundation

Cindy Carson
Social Solutions

Farron Levy
True Impact

Meg Plantz
United Way of America

External Reviewers List

Jon Quigley
Advanced Investment Partners

Melissa Janis
Alcoa Foundation

C. B. Bhattacharya
Boston University and European School
of Management and Technology

John Damonti
Bristol-Myers Squibb Company

Kat Rosqueta
Center for High Impact Philanthropy,
University of Pennsylvania

Ray Fisman
Columbia University

Lalita Advani
Credit Suisse

Bo Miller
The Dow Chemical Company

Gail Gershon
Gap Inc.

Michael Bzdak
Johnson & Johnson

Christine Petrovits
New York University

Caroline Roan
Pfizer Inc

Sarah Lem
RBC Capital Markets

Jeff Mason
Social Solutions and Alliance for Effective
Social Investing

We are also deeply grateful to the CECP Board of Directors for sharing invaluable insights and encouragement in this project and to Edwin Lee, 2009 John C. Whitehead Summer Intern, who contributed considerably to our research on social impact assessment frameworks.